TRADITIONAL FARM BUILDINGS OF WILTSHIRE

Dedicated to
John Reis, farmer at Compton Bassett,
for his many years of supporting our work

Traditional Farm Buildings of Wiltshire

Pamela M. Slocombe

HOBNOB PRESS

for the

WILTSHIRE BUILDINGS RECORD

First published in the United Kingdom in 2025
on behalf of the Wiltshire Buildings Record
by The Hobnob Press, 8 Lock Warehouse, Severn Road, Gloucester GL1 2GA.
    www.hobnobpress.co.uk

British Library Cataloguing in Publication Data
A catalogue record for this book is available from the British Library.

ISBN 978-1-914407-90-1

Typeset in 10/12 pt Adobe Garamond Pro.
Typesetting and origination by John Chandler

The Wiltshire Buildings Record is a voluntary society and educational charity, with members in historic Wiltshire and beyond. The archive of the Record, gathered together since 1979 from fieldwork and from a variety of sources, covers over 18,500 sites representing buildings of all dates and types. The collection is housed at the Wiltshire & Swindon History Centre, Cocklebury Road, Chippenham, Wiltshire SN15 3QN, telephone 01249 705508, www.wiltshirebuildingsrecord.org.uk. It is open to the public on Tuesdays, 9 a.m. to 5 p.m. or by arrangement.

Also available from Wiltshire Buildings Record:

Wiltshire Farmhouses and Cottages 1500-1850	£6
Medieval Houses of Wiltshire	£6
Wiltshire Town Houses 1500-1900	£6
Architects and Building Craftsmen with Work in Wiltshire (Part 1)	£5
Architects and Craftsmen with Work in Wiltshire (Part 2)	£5
Wiltshire Village Reading Rooms (Ivor Slocombe)	£8
Wiltshire Gate Lodges (James Holden)	£8
All plus £2 per copy post and packing.	
The Dovecotes and Pigeon Lofts of Wiltshire (J & P McCann)	reduced to £5
Wiltshire Almshouses and their Founders (Sally Thomson)	£10.50
Wiltshire Nonconformist Chapels and Meeting Houses (James Holden)	£20
Civic Pride: the Public Buildings of Wiltshire Towns (James Holden)	£20
All plus £4 per copy post and packing	

You can help the Record by allowing us to copy photographs, drawings and any other information, structural or historical you may have about Wiltshire buildings. Please join the Record and help to record buildings in your locality or assist us by drawing our attention to threatened buildings which may be worth recording.

Contents

Introduction

S INCE 'WILTSHIRE FARM *Buildings 1500-1900*' was published in 1989, the archive of the Wiltshire Buildings Record, now at the History Centre, Chippenham, has substantially increased. This new edition again uses material gleaned during fieldwork. There are ever more pressures on farmers to convert old unused agricultural buildings and in the process features are inevitably lost. We have provided, too, a home for the large number of records of farm buildings in the south-west of the county, made in the 1990s by students of the University of Bournemouth and co-ordinated by Carol Ryan. This was called the South West Wiltshire Rural Development Area Non-domestic Building Survey. The aim was to identify redundant buildings presenting opportunities for developing employment space.

In 2008 we launched a specific project to record farm buildings with the aid of grants from a farming member and Kennet District Council. New volunteers were recruited and this project still continues. We also took part in around 2014 in an English Heritage project to characterise farming areas. This has resulted in a number of guidance booklets.

The collection of material is now substantial. Yet despite the continued and increasing loss of traditional buildings, there still remain many farms in the county with buildings displaying very interesting features, relics of old farming practices. We are always looking for keen volunteers to help us record them.

Please note:
It must be strongly emphasised that most of the buildings mentioned in this book are on private land and very many have subsequently been altered or demolished. If readers are interested in a particular building, we recommend that in the first instance they consult Wiltshire Buildings Record for further information.

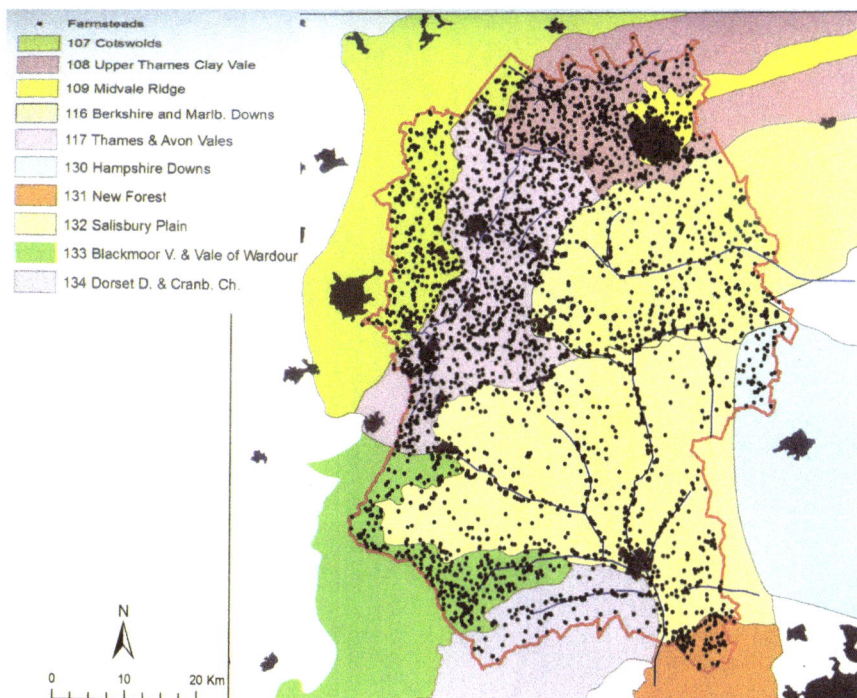

The farming areas of Wiltshire (Courtesy Edwards & Lake).

The Historical Background to Farming in Wiltshire

IN THE MEDIEVAL period the standard holding of one virgate or yardland comprised about 28 acres which was ploughland in scattered acre strips in the common fields and an allocation of hay meadow, often also held in common and shared out each year by lot, and a small amount of pasture land, often including a croft behind the house. The farmer also had a right to use rough grazing available on common and waste land.

A farm of this size probably only had a small multipurpose barn. A number of processes - dairying, malting, brewing - were carried out in the farmhouse itself. Manor houses with their demesne land required a larger range of farm buildings. Much of the county was in monastic estates and the wealth of the monasteries enabled excellent farm buildings to be erected for tenants' use. Some of these, especially the great barns, still survive. Some lay landlords also built well for their own demesne farms but their tenants were less well provided..

When the monasteries were dissolved in the first half of the 16th century, there was large scale redistribution of their lands. The Crown sold first to a small number of men who acquired large estates, particularly Edward Seymour. They then sold some of this on to lesser men and many of the manors were sold to the wealthy clothiers.

The manor houses were modernised with ceilings and fireplaces inserted but there may not have been much rebuilding of the farm buildings until the early 17th century. In the 16th and early 17th centuries many of the tenants' holdings still had medieval allocations of land but the tendency to amalgamate smaller holdings and rent out demesne land increased. Farms gradually changed from mixed agriculture to greater specialisation and there was the division of the county into two main areas often referred to as the chalk and the cheese. Enclosure of the open fields, enabled by the exchange of plots, was a gradual process from the 16th century onwards in the 'cheese', the parts of the county which specialised in cattle. There, small closes of pasture were desirable but it came late in the 'chalk', the sheep and corn areas.

In the mid-17th century the period of unrest during the Civil War put a halt to most building. However, from the late 17th century and on through the 18th century, farmyards received much attention. This does not seem to be true for all counties but a large number of farm buildings of this period survive in Wiltshire. Factors providing additional income were no doubt the cheese-making industry and periods of wealth in the woollen trade.

In the 18th century very large estates were again being accumulated, this time by the gentry. They were administered by agents who often imposed a common style of architecture on the holdings. In the 19th century this practice developed to an even greater extent with many estate farmyards being designed by agents or architects.

The end of the 18th century was a period when great emphasis was placed on improvements of all kinds in agriculture. The provision of good quality purpose-built buildings was part of this. There was also further consolidation of farms during this period. Davis, writing in 1794, mentions that where three or four estates in South Wiltshire were rented by one farmer 'all the farm-houses except one, are let to labourers, and great part of the outbuildings are suffered to go to decay'. Many of today's 'cottages' were once farmhouses.

There is some evidence that the provision of farm buildings in Wiltshire was traditionally the responsibility of the landowner. One set of estate accounts of the late 17th century regularly notes the building or repair of tenants' buildings. Davis confirms this in his sections on South and North Wiltshire but noted that thatching was usually left to the tenant in the south.

Sources

A USEFUL ACCOUNT of the development of the county's agriculture in general and in the specialised areas is given in vol. 4 of the *Victoria County History of Wiltshire*. An overview of developments in the medieval period can be found in John Hare's *A Prospering Society*. For the 17th century Joe Bettey's *Wiltshire Farming in the Seventeenth Century* is unrivalled. It provides a wide selection of original sources with a commentary. Peter Stanier's *Wiltshire in the Age of Steam* describes the gradual mechanisation of farming in the 18th and 19th centuries. For a firsthand account of the situation in the late 18th and early 19th centuries, Thomas Davis's *General View of the Agriculture of Wiltshire* of 1794, revised in 1811, is invaluable. For the late 19th century the extensive books and articles by Richard Jefferies describe farming methods and buildings in the area round Swindon.

There are a number of useful sources for the study of individual farms. For the early part of the period the inventories which accompanied wills often list the farm buildings with their contents of animals and equipment. Marriage settlements sometimes give good detail when properties were being divided. Wiltshire's glebe terriers (surveys by the church authorities of their lands), were published in vol. 56 of the Wiltshire Record Society. They describe parsonage farms, often giving the building materials of the farm buildings and their size either in measurements or the number of bays or fields (roof sections) of building. The *Surveys of Lord Pembroke's Manors 1631-2,* also published by the Wiltshire Record Society, gives a wealth of detail about ordinary copyhold farms in a number of parishes, mostly in the south of the county but it also includes Stanton St Bernard and West Overton.

Newspaper advertisements and sale particulars of the 19th century frequently give detailed information about buildings, equipment and stock. The extensive sales of large estates in the county around 1900 are covered by ample catalogues sometimes with photographs of the farmyards as well as the farmhouses. Copies of these catalogues can be consulted at the Wiltshire & Swindon History Centre and the library of Wiltshire Museum, Devizes.

The late 19th century Ordnance Survey maps at a scale of 25 inches to the mile are invaluable and provide information on many buildings which have gone. Buildings are shown in plan with dotted lines for open fronts, indicating cart sheds and shelter sheds. Barns are distinguishable by their size and often by porches. Pigsties are evident from the adjoining enclosures.

The Inland Revenue Land Valuation field books of 1911 in the National Archives at Kew have maps of farms and other details pre-first world war.

Cases during that war were documented in '*First World War Tribunals in Wiltshire*' by Ivor Slocombe for Wiltshire Family History Society. Sons and farm hands were 'applied for' to prevent their being conscripted and this gives many details about the farm. For example at Pittsland Farm, Brinkworth, W.C. Rumming had 238 acres with 52 cows in full milk, 38 in-calf cows and other cattle, 25 pigs, 16 sheep in June and about 150 in the autumn. He expected to mow 100 acres. One man had joined the army and three more had joined since war broke out. He had female labour for milking cows but they did not milk on Sundays or in the evening. There were six milkers for 60 cows.

Farming methods were required to change during World War II. The book *Odlum v Stratton* is the record of a case about a farm at Manningford Bohun, near Pewsey. The farmer contended that his way of farming suited the soil conditions on certain parts of the farm and that ploughing up would be harmful. There was also a further National Farm Survey in 1941-3.

Farming Methods

S OME KNOWLEDGE OF farming methods is important for a better understanding of farm buildings. A few of the general features of Wiltshire farming will be mentioned here.

The woollen and cloth industries led to the keeping of very large numbers of sheep and many lands were over-stocked from the medieval period onwards. The downland was particularly favoured for grazing and sheep were often kept with another farmer on the downs far away from the valley farm where they were owned.

Manure from the sheep improved the quality of the arable land on the slopes of the downs where they were folded at night. Cows also grazed certain areas of the downs as part of a seasonal rotation. The water meadows in the valleys were used for spring grazing and for hay making. In the south-east of the county, sluices enabled controlled flooding of the meadows in spring to bring on early grass for the sheep, and cows were fed on the after-grass. The Avon valley in the north-west of the county had particularly rich pastures which were used for fattening Welsh cattle in the 16th and 17th centuries. The landlord might lease his land to a tenant and lend him money at interest for the purchase of stock. The tenant then took the risk of the enterprise. The growth of dairying in this area from the late 17th century until its peak in the late 19th century caused a greater requirement for cowsheds than in many other parts of the country and many fine examples with stone or brick pillared fronts survive.

As so much labour was involved in dairy work, rented dairying was widely practised, as explained by J. H. Bettey in *Rural Life in Wessex 1500-1900*. This went beyond the lending of money by landlords. The farmers owned dairy cows which they rented out annually to a dairyman. The farmer also provided pasture and hay, and a house and dairy. This is the reason for the number of holdings called 'Dairy Farm', 'Dairy', 'Dey House' or 'Milk House' in the county. The dairyman paid an annual rent per cow and earned his living by selling the milk, butter and cheese. The farmer could then limit his own farming to corn and sheep.

During the late 19th century, improvements in transport meant that dairy farms could concentrate on milk production only, the milk being processed in local factories or sent to the towns. A by-product of cheese-making was whey. This was fed to pigs which provided further income and a bacon industry which was concentrated on Calne, Chippenham and Trowbridge. This continued until relatively recently. The county has therefore got larger numbers of pigsties and of earlier date than in counties with a chiefly arable economy.

The medieval method of ploughing by oxen was still widely used in Wiltshire in the 16th century. After this date horses were increasingly used especially on light soil. The oxhouse gradually gave way to the carthorse stable, often using the same building. The last oxen were, surprisingly, still in use in the early 20th century and there are several photographs of teams including two young men with a team of three at Aldbourne in Corfield *A Guide to the Industrial Archaeology of Wiltshire*.

Grain was a major product over large areas of the county and was locally stored in barns in preference to ricks. Davis said the complaint was often made that Wiltshire corn instead of being dry and slippery was moist and rough because it had not dried out sufficiently. There is some evidence of corn-drying in kilns, usually those next to the kitchen fireplace which were also used for bacon-curing.

Poultry do not figure prominently in inventories, perhaps because they were often a side line of the farmer's wife. An exception is the large Hilperton farm of Christopher Smith where in 1592 he had nine geese, twelve ducks and thirty hens. The farm was sited next to a large common. Usually where poultry are mentioned the numbers are smaller. The county did not have the large areas of marshland which favoured the keeping of flocks of geese but this is known to have been practised in the Avon valley around Broughton Gifford. Pigeons, however, were kept in large numbers in the arable areas judging by the architectural evidence of dovecotes and pigeon lofts. These are fully described in John McCann's *The Dovecotes and Pigeon Lofts of Wiltshire.*

Orchards tended to be small, providing fruit for home consumption. Cider was made on a small scale but beer was the chief drink. There is evidence of hop growing in the 17th century, particularly in the Swindon area and in the sandy soils near Calne and Bromham but also in the south of the county. Little Cheverell Rectory had a hop garden in around.1600. No hop-drying kilns have been found so presumably malting kilns were used or the hops were hung to dry in attics or out of doors.

Market gardening suited some of the greensand areas and was practised especially around Devizes and Bromham and in the Warminster and Westbury areas but it, too, does not seem to have led to the survival of specialist buildings there. There is documentary evidence for a 'coppice barn' at Bradford-on-Avon built on four acres of oak coppice which the 'slaymaker' bought in 1734 to store the wood he used in the making of looms. There were also bark barns at tanneries to store the bark used in the tanning of hides, such as one at Lacock.

The Sites and the Size of Farms

HISTORICAL RESEARCH SUGGESTS that many of the isolated farms in the countryside, accompanied usually by a few farm cottages, represent the most ancient pattern of settlement in England, dating back to the Anglo-Saxon period and beyond. The grouping of farms in villages was largely a medieval development.

At all periods since the Saxon, however, new farms have been created on new sites where a block of land could be obtained. Methods have included the clearance of woodland, the enclosure of common or waste land or the enclosure or purchase of a group of small fields formed out of the strips of the great medieval open fields of the village. Some examples of isolated farms recorded by Wiltshire Buildings Record are Cove House Farm, The Leigh (an ancient freehold from at least the 13th century), Burton Grove Farm, South Marston (with place-name evidence since 1327); Rhotteridge Farm, Melksham Without (probably on land enclosed from Melksham Forest, early 17th century), Brights Farm, Christian Malford (from former 'waste' of the manor in the late 18th century), Widbrook Farm, Bradford-on-Avon (from open fields 1834-5).

Ancient freeholds, otherwise known as 'reputed manors', were freehold estates with extensive lands (two virgates – a half hide- or more) held under a main manor. The holders were gentry and the house therefore had similar status to a manor house and usually boasted very good quality farm buildings. The occupant was often a leaseholder under the freeholder.

The requirements of an isolated farm site have not changed through the ages; a water supply, a sheltered aspect and good land. In the late 18th and early 19th centuries a good view or 'prospect' became fashionable for houses though it must always have been less important for a farm. Davis said that farms in the south of Wiltshire were 'in general crowded together in the villages, for the conveniency of water …'.

The lack of shelter and the downland soil 'too light, and too thin' as Davis said, discouraged the siting of farms on the exposed areas of the chalk downs, Salisbury Plain and the Marlborough Downs. Any farms on the downs were in the valley bottoms, the position, for example, that the now deserted village of Imber occupied.

Some isolated farms have never been accompanied by more than one or two cottages but some are former manor houses once surrounded by small villages. Sheldon Manor, Chippenham Without, Brook House Farm at Heywood, Rowden Farm at Lacock, and Cloatley Manor at Hankerton had by the 19th century all descended from great medieval houses to working, tenanted farms.

Before the enclosure of common land in the late 18th and early 19th centuries almost every dweller in the countryside had some land, including tradesmen, innkeepers and the clergy. The use of former farmhouses in villages as labourers' cottages has been already mentioned. Though some houses remained as farms until the end of the 19th century or later, most have now long since become private houses. Some of the farm buildings sited adjoining village houses remain though they are gradually disappearing. Some were converted for use by tradesmen (for example, carpenters), some were converted to separate houses at an early date and some were used for general storage. Some examples are Thorn House, Steeple Ashton (the stable converted to a house extension), Queen Elizabeth Cottage, Broad Town (the barn partly fallen down and the remainder converted), Webbs Farm, Chiseldon (the barn used by a carpenter and undertaker), Manor Farm, Broad Blunsdon (the brewhouse used as a garage). Sometimes a nearby outbuilding has become part of the house by the building of a link section between. This has been the case at Leigh House Farm, Bradford-on-Avon (a bakehouse later joined to the farmhouse), Wallmead Farm, Tisbury (a brewhouse joined) and Ridge Farm, Neston, Corsham (an out-kitchen joined).

The Farm Buildings –Some General Remarks

I N SPITE OF the great diversity of appearance of farm buildings in the county, the function of each one can usually be deduced from its form. The exceptions to this are those few which have been greatly altered and extensively repaired several times and can now only be described as outbuildings.

It has always been common to build dual purpose or multipurpose buildings. This can sometimes confuse the recorder but the different functions were usually in separate sections of the building which was divided either horizontally, vertically, or in both ways.

The farmhouse itself was often multi-purpose. The longhouse, for example, only used in the early medieval period in Wiltshire, combined living quarters with a cattle stall under one roof. Dairying was originally carried out in the hall (the main living room) or the kitchen and only at a later date was provision made in a lean-to or a special room or wing. The house might also have a cheeseroom on the first floor, an attached brewhouse, and a granary or doveloft in the roof. In north-west Wiltshire in the 18th century the barn might be attached to the farmhouse. Some of these uses of the farmhouse are illustrated in *Wiltshire Farmhouses and Cottages 1500-1850*. This present book concentrates on detached or semi-detached farm buildings but a few of these incorporated living accommodation for farm workers.

Interesting farm buildings can be found all over the county but in the north-west and central areas the early wealth from wool and from cheese in the 18th and early 19th centuries, led to the construction of particularly well-built farm buildings. In these areas there was also a supply of good stone and wood and this also has led to the survival of more early buildings than can be found in some other parts of the country.

Some farm buildings were always more important than others. This is reflected in the quality of their construction. Good riding horses and pigeons were status symbols in the early part of the period and this was reflected in better architectural details on some stables and dovecotes compared with, say, cowsheds and pigsties. However, on the model farms of the large estates there can be matching detailing on all the buildings.

Dereliction and conversion have always happened, particularly when times were hard or the estate became run down through the circumstances of the owner. Since the late 20th century, however, we have seen probably the greatest reduction in the number of farmsteads since the one which Thomas Davis described at the time of enclosure in South Wiltshire in the late 18th century. Good farm buildings were usually constructed as an investment in a period of farming prosperity and were used and repaired over a long period until either farming methods changed or new ownership lead to a complete renewal. Hardly any new 'model farms' have been built since the break-up of most of the large estates in the early 20th century. Today a proportion of most farmsteads is in some state of dereliction. Repairs of the traditional buildings are not usually made with the original materials but with the cheapest effective material of the day. Geoffrey Grigson described the first use of corrugated iron in the late-19th century to repair thatch. Where traditional buildings survive they are mainly used for storage whilst the main work of the farm takes place in large modern units.

The Types of Buildings

THE DOCUMENTARY SOURCES mentioned above tell us what sorts of buildings there were on Wiltshire farms. Most 16th century inventories do not mention farm buildings. When they do there is often only a barn. The following examples are from different areas and periods. They are the farmsteads of manors, parsonages or large farmers. Their poorer neighbours would have had fewer buildings and many farms had only a multi-purpose barn. It is interesting to see, from these limited examples, how the number of farm buildings on a holding tended to increase over time.

Barton Farm, Bradford-on-Avon, 1367, dairy, brewhouse, malthouse, granary, great barn, little barn, bailiff's stable, cart house and dovecote (round the main yard), also an oxhouse and a carthorse stable (probably in a second yard).

Bewley Court, Lacock, 1548, 'a gardyner (granary) for corne conteyning on(e) room, a stable of iii romes, a berton and a ga(r)don and an o(r)chard'.

From *Wiltshire Glebe Terriers 1588-1827* (WRS, vol.56):

Rectory, Baverstock, 1609, a kitchen severed from the dwelling house, with milk house, bolting house, malt loft, a barn of 7 rooms together with stalls, stables, sheep houses, cart house, with other houses for swine and poultry.

Vicarage, Ashton Keynes, 1611, a barn of roughstone, slated upon the top, being 5 space beside the porch, every space being 10 feet in length, Stable and oxhouse of 10 spaces covered in thatch.

The following six extracts are from Glebe Terriers of 1649, all in *Wiltshire Archaeological Magazine (WAM) vol. 15*:

Rectory, Sherston, 'two barnes covered with tyle, one dove loft over the porch of one of the said barnes, one stable, one oxhouse, one waine house covered with thatch in all conteyning sixteene bayes of buildinge'.

Rectory, Sutton Benger, 'two Barnes of 10 Bayes of building, a Stable and a heyhouse of 4 bayes of building'.

Rectory, Swallowcliffe, 'a Barne and stable of five Bayes of buildinge'.

St Sampson's Rectory, Cricklade 'a barne of six bayes of buildinge, a stable and oxhouse of four bayes, a wainhouse, two gardens, a courtyard and a Rickbarton'.

Rectory, Collingbourne Kingston with a 'very faire Mansion house', 'three Barnes, one Fodder house, three stables, a dove house well stored and other outhousings'.

Rectory, Preshute, 'two Barnes conteyning two Bayes of buildinge, two stabeles conteyninge two Bayes of buildinge, a carthouse, a cow staall'.

Rectory, Keevil, 'one large Barne built with Stone & Timber and covered with stone slate'.

Various later examples are interesting to compare:

1671 Parsonage House, Trowbridge, 'one Tiled Barn with a stall at the end of it, a Dovehouse and Pigsty adjoining. One Thatcht Barne with a Stable at the end of it. Another pigsty and an Henhouse'. Glebe Terrier, WAM 15 p.226.

1695 deed. Frankley (later Maplecroft) Farm, Bradford-onAvon. 'An ancient barn, new barn to the North of the old barn, sheephouse to its South. Pigeonhouse. Cornhouse and whitehouse. Oxhouse. Killing house. Great Barton and Pig Barton, henhouse.'

1715 deed. Capital mansion house at Winsley. 'Barn, oxhouse, stables, wainhouse and other outhouses.'

1783 Rectory, North Wraxall, 'Two Barns built with stone and covered with thatch, one 57 long and 18 wide, the other 38 foot long and 17 wide, three stables, one three-staled, the other two-staled, and other an old one & has not been used as a Stable for many years, all built with stone & covered with thatch. A Coach House and Greanery over built with stone & covered with tile. A Cart House covered with thatch'. Glebe Terrier in Lewis *History of the Parish of North Wraxall.*

1783 Rectory, Castle Combe, a brewhouse built with stone covered partly with stone and partly with thatch, a barn 60 feet by 20 feet built with stone and covered with tile, a stable built with stone and covered with thatch, large enough for 6 horses, a granary built with stone and covered with tile.

1898 sale particulars. Manor House, Steeple Langford, ' Brick and slate coach house and open shed. Cob and thatch coal house. Range of timber and thatch stabling consisting of loose box, harness room, chaff house and stable for 11 horses. Timber and tile chaff house and 3 loose boxes. Brick and thatch chaff house. Timber and thatch open cattle shed. Timber and thatch cow house for 15 cows. Two piggeries with feeding passage. Timber and thatch implement shed. Large corn store and mixing floor. Timber and slate granary on stone saddles. Fowl house. Timber and slate open cow shed for 10 cows. Two 4-bay timber and slate open sheds. Root house. 5-bay open shed with corrugated iron roof. 6-bay brick and slate cart shed. Timber and slate cart shed. Stone and slate nag stable with 3 loose boxes and harness room.'

The barns mentioned at Cricklade in 1649 and Bradford-on-Avon in 1695 were medieval cruck barns, already very old then. The former survived until the 20th century and the latter still exists, converted to residential use. The Steeple Langford farm in 1898 had 690 acres in the parish, part downland and part pasture including water meadow. The buildings were arranged around two yards.

Building Materials and Techniques

THE FARM BUILDINGS were usually built more cheaply than the farmhouses and old-fashioned styles and methods lingered on for centuries after they had been discarded for dwellings. This often makes the study of farm buildings especially interesting. Aisled construction was abandoned at an early date in houses but continued in barns which are open to the rafters as open halls had been and windbraces were used in barn roofs until a later date than in houses. Stables show the use of outside stairs, cobbled floors and shuttered, unglazed windows. Brewhouses developed from the detached kitchens of the medieval period and still retained downhearth cooking during the 19th century when it had gone from all but the very poorest houses. Wiltshire cowsheds and stables sometimes had bratticed (staggered plank) partitions at a date when they were no longer used in houses. Monolithic windows were an old technique kept longer in outbuildings. In an area with chalk stone, timber or brick houses, the outbuildings were still often of cob, a more ancient material, called 'mud' in documents. Some cob still survives today but it is becoming rarer. Until relatively recently farm buildings were commonly thatched. All the 18th century buildings with half-hipped roofs are likely to have been thatched. There is evidence of stone tiling being used for some of the roofs of farm buildings belonging to important manor houses in the medieval period. The Malmesbury Abbey record of buildings constructed by Abbot William who died in 1296 distinguishes those stone tiled from those thatched. For example, at Crudwell he constructed '*unam grangiam magnam petra coopertam et aliam grangiam stramine coopertam, quae appellatur Putbarn*' – a large barn, stone-roofed and another barn, thatched, called Putbarn.

Another early material was solid thatch. There were no roof trusses and brushwood was piled on top of flat joists and then thatched. It may have once been used for humble houses but continued in use for some farm buildings. A feed rack, sheephouse and cartshed made like this are described below. There are now few if any examples of the practice left in Wiltshire.

Carpentry which can help with dating

SOME TYPES OF roof construction were more suitable for farm buildings than for houses. This was especially true of sling brace roof trusses which gave more headroom permitting movement along the centre of a loft. They are found especially in stables and granaries. They date from the late 18th century to the early 19th century.

Other roof types which dominate in farm buildings are the various types of queen strut roofs which were used especially in barns, and king post roofs, especially found in 19th century cowsheds. Queen struts, either raking (slanting) or straight, above the tiebeam might be used either with or without an upper collar. The king post gave good support to the ridge piece which took most of the weight of the roof covering when only a single row of purlins was used along each side of the roof. Variations in the 19th century were the strapped king post, the king bolt truss and the king rod truss. The latter was specified for a farmstead on Salisbury Plain in 1863.

Queen post trusses were in use for a shorter period concentrated on the 1830s but continuing till the 1850s.

Sling braces; Manor Farm, Chilton Foliat, Mount Sorrel Farm, Broad Chalke, Chapel Farm, Blunsdon.

left: Raking queen struts with clasped purlins, Village Farm, Cholderton. right: Straight queen struts, Brazen Bottom Farm, West Lavington.

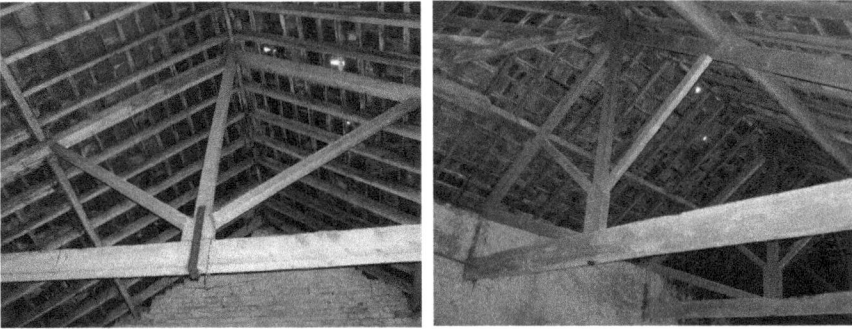

left: Strapped king post truss, Netherhampton Farm, Netherhampton.
right: King bolt truss, Manor Farm, Chitterne.

left: King rod truss, Ugford Farm, Burcombe Without.
right: Queen post truss, Chase Woods Farm, Aldbourne.

Where timber-framing was used, jowled posts may assist dating. This is the thickening at the head to receive both the tiebeam of the roof truss and the wallplate running along the top of the wall. Different shapes were preferred at different periods. Seven types of jowl in East Kent barns were identified by F. Brown in an article in *Vernacular Architecture, vol. 7.* They varied over time but the periods when they were popular overlap.

A Wiltshire sequence has not yet been fully determined and the suggested dating below is from Brown.

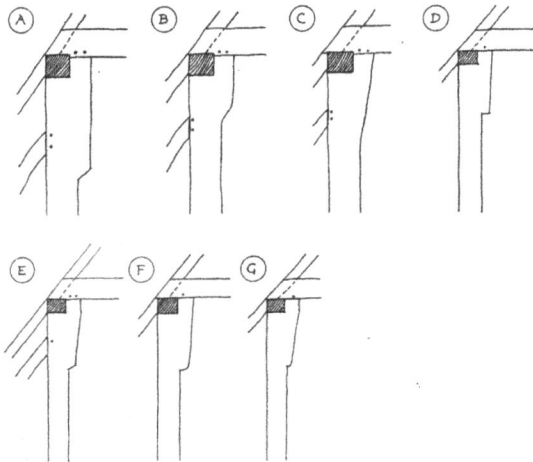

Jowled posts (F. Brown).

Type a is a long jowl, sharply cut in at the base, 1250-1430, predominantly 14th century

Type b is an adzed, roughly shaped jowl with no sharp angle, bellied out, 1350 to 1650-1700

Type c is adzed with no sharp angle and gradual thickening, 1350 to 1650-1750 (But 1767 at the granary at A'Becketts, West Lavington)

Type d is sawn, with a straight or sloping head and sharp, right-angled return, 1600-1750

Type e is sawn with a sharp diagonal return, 1630-1750 or later

Type f is sawn with a convex moulding, 1740-1860

Type g is sawn with a narrower jowl, 1740-1880

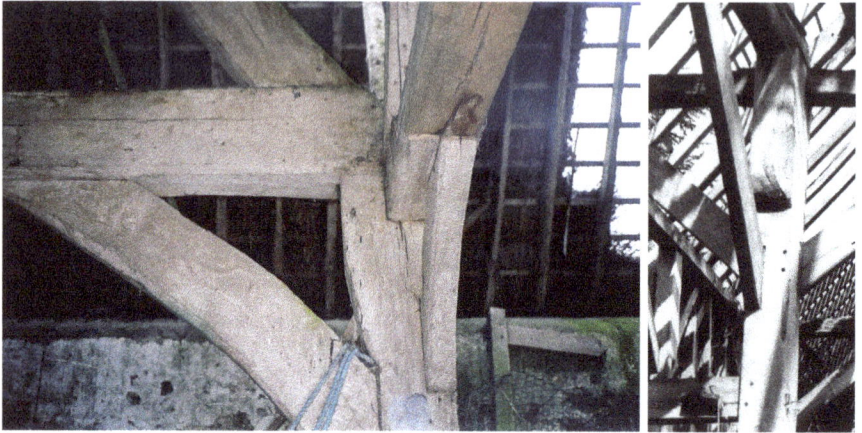

Type b, North Farm, West Overton and Village Farm, Cholderton (very bellied out).

Type e, Chase Woods Farm, Aldbourne.

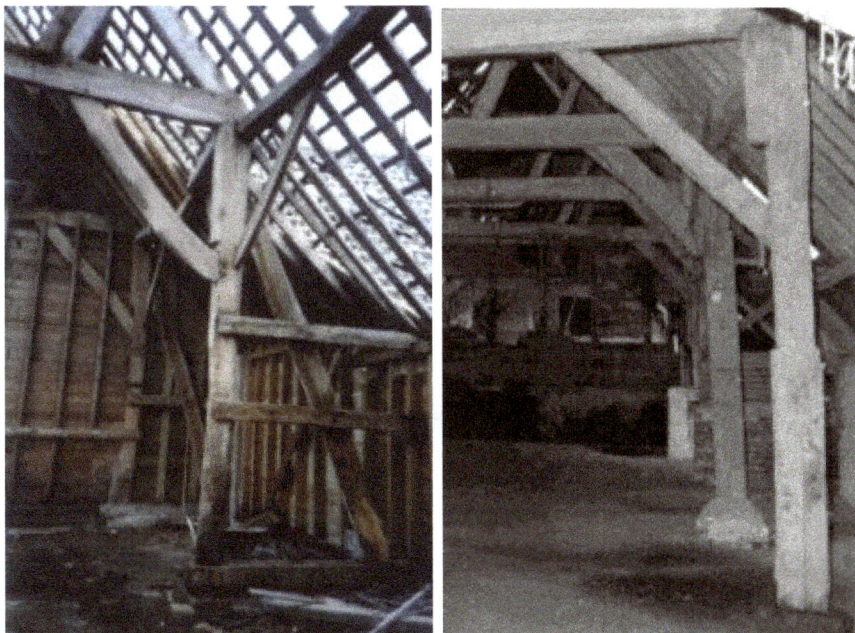

left: Type d, Park farm, Chilton Foliat.
right: Type f, West Kennett Farm, Avebury.

The Layout of the Farm

FROM THE MEDIEVAL period onwards the ideal layout of the farm buildings, where the owner could afford it, seems to have been a courtyard, or series of courtyards. This gave the advantages of security, protection from the weather and a compact working unit. It also gave a visually pleasing and imposing effect. Barton Farm at Bradford-on-Avon is a good early example of this though the buildings were not all constructed at the same time. The manor house stands on the north side of the yard shielding it from the colder winds, the great barn is at the opposite end giving an architectural balance, on the east side of the yard is the granary with, formerly. pigsties, the dairy, malthouse and brewhouse and on the west side was an older, smaller barn. All the buildings were strongly constructed of best quality timber, and later stone, so that though the farm was built under the Abbey of Shaftesbury's ownership, many of the buildings have survived until today.

When Sir William Sharington purchased Lacock Abbey in 1540, following the Dissolution, he rebuilt the stableyard using the courtyard plan and including a brewhouse and other service buildings.

John Aubrey wrote in about 1670 of Bradfield, Hullavington: 'The House is of the old gothic fashion with the barne within the court, which was the general way of building the Mansion howses of the Lords of Mannors.'

Most farms with more than one yard started out with buildings around a single yard and a second yard was added in the 19th century to provide ranges of cowsheds. Thomas Davis said that in South Wiltshire there was usually a straw-yard for the cattle with buildings around.

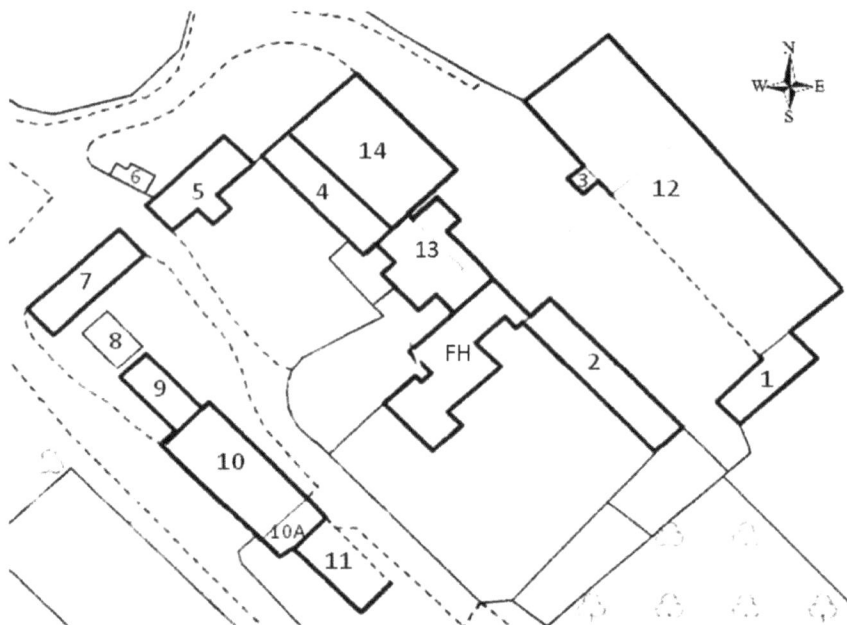

Rodmead Farm, Maiden Bradley. 1 waggon shed, 2 milking shed, 3 pigsty and hen house, 4 modern, 5. carthorse stable, 6 smithy and privy, 7 cowshed, 8 granary, 9 nag stable, 10 barn, 11 cart shed, 12-14 modern.

In the strawyard manure accumulated which was later spread on the fields. It is evident from descriptions of properties that there was also usually a rick yard or 'rick barton' adjoining the barn where some of the crops were stored in ricks. 'Court' and 'barton' were old words for a yard (hence Barton Farm mentioned above) and the area of yard directly behind the house was called the 'backside'.

'Model farms', with the house and outbuildings all of one period, are associated particularly with the late 18th and 19 centuries but they could be built at any date. The wealth of the owner was the key factor as it was very expensive to build a whole farmstead at one time. We find the remnants of a few such early farms today but the odds are against their having survived intact as the lesser buildings would always have been less well constructed.

Some examples are Belle Cour Farm, Wingfield (early 18th century), New Farm, Lacock (early 18th century), Lower Hardenhuish Farm, Langley Burrell Without (New Farm on an estate map of 1775), Widbrook Farm, Bradford-on-Avon (1834-5) and Trimnells Farm, Colerne (about 1874). All these were built by estate owners. The farmyard buildings at Chilton House, Chilton Foliat, were mostly erected around 1773.

Even more elaborate farmsteads with open and covered yards were built by the owners of the very largest estates, particularly in the 19th century. For example, Stall (formerly Oxstalls) Farm (1859) and Park Farm (1860) at Horningsham, both designed by William Wilkinson, an Oxford architect, for Longleat, and Netherhampton Farm, Netherhampton (c. 1862), Bemerton Farm (late 1850s) and Little Langford, Steeple Langford (1865-6). Netherhampton was designed by the agent with the architect Samuel Clarke of Salisbury for Wilton House. In 1872 the Wilton estate was the largest in Wiltshire and throughout the 19th century a great deal of capital was spent on improving its farms. In 1920 Little Langford was described as 'all elaborately and substantially built of stone with slated roofs, ... one of the finest homesteads in the county.'

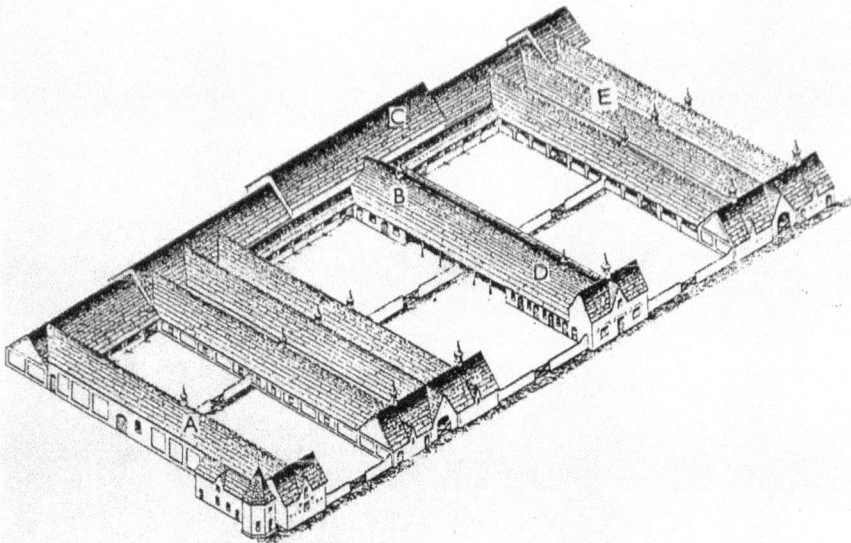

Netherhampton Farm, c. 1862. A stables for 14 horses B fattening boxes C barn D piggery E covered yards for dairy cattle.

The desire for a good appearance was well expressed in Joseph Gwilt's *Encyclopaedia of Architecture* of 1867. He advised that the farmyard despite the 'seemingly repulsive nature of the subject ... may be made very picturesque'.

Many small farms did not have enough buildings to complete the four sides of a yard or had only buildings of different periods, replaced from time to time. Geoffrey Grigson commented on the uncontrived but attractive appearance of such randomly built farms in the Swindon area;

And if one stands back, and looks at the whole assembly of the farm and its buildings, at their arrangement one against another, their placing in the landscape ... if one considers them in time as well as spatially, in their kinship to generation after generation of farmers and farm-workers, and manorial lords and landlords, one must again realise how little this agreeableness has come by conscious effort.

Even apparently random farmsteads usually conform to one of several types. In 'dispersed plans' there is no principal yard but the buildings are scattered alongside a through route. This is common in nucleated villages. 'Loose courtyard' describes the buildings developed in piecemeal fashion around a cattle yard with cart and waggon sheds placed around the perimeter facing routes and tracks. The farmhouse is typically detached. In 'regular courtyard plans', mostly of 19th century date ,the buildings are in linked ranges arranged in a full courtyard, L-, U-, or E- plan with one or more yards for the collection of manure. Several of the Wilton estate farms have the E-plan. In 'parallel plans' the buildings lie opposite the farmhouse which may have a dairy and brewhouse attached to it. There are also 'linear plans' with the buildings strung out in a line but these are more common in northern or western pastoral areas of the country. There are also isolated buildings or outfarms which include sheephouses, cowsheds and field barns. These are very common on the downland but are also found in other parts of the county.

E plan, Little Langford Farm, Steeple Langford.

An analysis of the dates of construction of farm buildings on a farm, if it is not a 'model farm', usually reveals that periods of rebuilding and repair of the farm buildings are paralleled by alterations to the farmhouse. This is probably because a landlord would repair and improve the whole farmstead during a vacancy in the hope of attracting a good new tenant.

Eastrop Farm, Highworth, a model farm.

Sometimes either the farmhouse or the farm buildings have been completely replaced leaving the other intact. Reasons for this might be that the farmhouse burnt down or that the farm buildings got into such a state of dereliction that they had to be totally replaced. At Lower Easton Farm, Corsham most of the farm buildings are 19th century, apart from an 18th century barn and stable near the road but the house dates back to about 1600. At Church Farm, Atworth the barn is medieval but the farmhouse probably dates from the 19th century.

Farmyard Features

Walls and gateposts

IN WILTSHIRE THE walls reflect the local cheapest building materials and may be of limestone, sarsen, cob and thatch, flint, chalk, brick or a mixture of these.

left:Sarsen yard wall, West Kennett Farm, Avebury right: Limestone gate post, Widbrook Farm, Bradford-on-Avon.

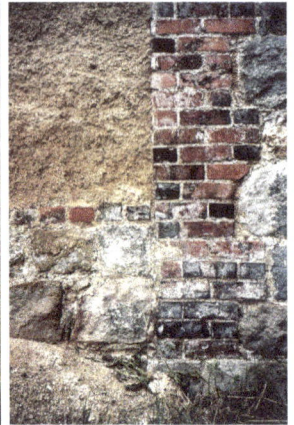

left: Dudmore Lodge, Aldbourne, sarsen and brick wall
right: Brick quoins to sarsen stable wall with inscribed date 1802 and adjoining building with a cob wall over a sarsen and brick plinth, North Farm, West Overton.

Walling, Salisbury plain farm, a type of concrete consisting of small flints and chalk with a high proportion of mortar, rendered both sides. This was used also for the farm buildings. Before 1887.

Some yards were cobbled. This was the case at Pinnells Farm, Brinkworth.

Pinnells Farm, Brinkworth in 1955 with a feeder covered with solid thatch and a cobbled yard (© Historic England Archive).

Water supply

A SOURCE OF water was essential and many farms were sited on the spring line. Others were sited on a stream or were provided with a stone-lined pond. Dewponds were constructed on the downs. A hollow was made in the chalk and lined with layers of clay and straw consolidated with a layer of lime. Certain families specialised in this work.

left: Pond at Lower Bridmore Farm, Donhead St. Mary.
right: A dew pond near Imber on Salisbury Plain in 1932 during a drought.

Wells could be dug almost anywhere. The shaft could have straight sides or be bottle-shaped. The lower part was usually left as natural rock with the top constructed of stone or brick. The well and the winding gear might be protected by a small cap or by a circular or square building. This could be enclosed or open-sided with the roof on posts or pillars. It might be protected by a pentice when close to a building. A wellhouse of brick with a thatched roof was described in a court case of 1918 and stood at Stonehenge Bottom, Amesbury. Increasingly from the 17th century a metal pump was provided and a small D-shaped or square stone trough. There were longer drinking troughs for the animals.

above left: Well capstone with slots for the
superstructure, Poplar Farm, Atworth
below left: Well at Ragge Farm, Colerne. The wall
is added.
right: Well house at Weavers Cottages,
Slaughterford, Biddestone, a former farm. By
tradition, wool was dried here and water drained
into a shallow 'dry well'.

Pumps;, Slate Farm, Wanborough with stone trough, Lower Bridmore Farm, Donhead St. Mary and Upper Combe Farm, Castle Combe.

Stone troughs; Manor Farm, Chitterne and Pinkney Court Farm, Sherston.

Deep wells on the chalk, which could be up to 360 feet deep, were sometimes powered by a donkey wheel. The first recorded example in England dates from 1587. Examples are known in Wiltshire at Lower Upham Farm, Aldbourne, Old Manor Farm, Broad Hinton (dismantled in 1908) and at New Farm, Stratford Toney (removed to the museum at Lackham). Another probable example was photographed by Peter Nicholson at Church Farm, Woodborough in around 1970. The wheels operated using two wooden or metal buckets which were attached to the axle so one was lowered as one was raised. On Salisbury Plain wind vanes provided power to some deep wells from the late 19th century and on the chalk downs small reservoirs were also constructed. Many are marked on O.S. maps of the area.

From the early 19th century horse gins were sometimes used for water supply. Some were made by Reeves of Bratton. Their records include one to raise water from a lake at Rood Ashton, West Ashton and one at Whaddon Farm, Hilperton to raise water from the river Avon.

Wheel houses: Old Manor Farm, Broad Hinton, Lower Upham Farm, Aldbourne and Church Farm, Woodborough.

Dog kennels

Dog kennels In the northern limestone part of the county these were sometimes under the outside stairs to granaries and lofts. Separate kennels are probably always of later date. At Folly Farm, Corsham a pair of brick kennels has round-arched doorways with a round window between. Separate kennels are probably always of later date. At Folly Farm, Corsham a pair of brick kennels has round-arched doorways with a round window between.

above left: Kennels under outside stairs: with a keeping hole above at Pinkney Court Farm, Sherston.
above right: At Starveall Farm, Chippenham Without.
below left: Folly Farm, Corsham.

Fodder

F ODDER IN THE yards was placed in a wooden or iron feed rack. Few of these have
survived. There was one in the yard of Home Farm, Roundway. The photograph
above of the yard at Pinnells Farm, Grittenham, Brinkworth shows an interesting
wooden example, with a solid thatch roof.

Bees

W HERE BEES WERE kept, the straw skeps were placed sometimes on bee stones
or in wall alcoves called bee boles, made for the purpose. These might be in the
farm garden where flowers were nearby. Bees are rarely mentioned in farm inventories.
One farm at Whaddon, Hilperton had a 'stall of bees' in 1649, another had 'two stalls
of bees' in1637 and a more prosperous farm at Lower Paxcroft in the same parish had
'five stocks of bees' in1631. The first farm was a half yardland, the second and third
were full yardlands (about 28 acres).

left: Bee stone at Poplar Farm, Atworth.
right: Skeps on beestones at St Fagan's Museum (R. Clark).

Brick beeboles at Widbrook Farm, Bradford-on-Avon. The farm dates from 1834-5.

left: Boles in the garden wall at Ridge Farm, Neston, Corsham.
right: Twenty beeboles in a semi-circular chalk wall roofed with thatch at Uffcott Farm,
Broad Hinton. Each opening is .43m wide, .32 - .37 m deep and .37 m high. They are
1.55 m above ground level, divided by brick piers and have flat backs. They were first
recorded in 1900.

Geese

At BROUGHTON GIFFORD where large flocks of geese were kept on the common, goose gates in the garden walls let the geese out to graze. They were kept by residents who were not all farmers.

Goose gates by the common at Broughton Gifford (R Clark).

Barns

IN POPULAR SPEECH the word 'barn' is used for any farm outbuilding but it properly applies to a building used to store and process grain crops or to store hay, peas or beans. The term 'tithe barn' is commonly used for any large, old barn but should only apply to barns used to store the tithes (tenth parts) of crops which were due to the church authorities in a parish, which was usually either the rector or an ecclesiastical lord of the manor.

Barns have at least one large high doorway in a side wall (not an end wall) and at least part of the building is open from floor to rafters. The large doorway always leads on to the threshing floor (or midsty) where farmworkers with flails or machinery removed the grain from the harvested crops.

Aisled barns

AISLED TIMBER-FRAMED BARNS are a 'lowland' type, concentrated in Kent and Hampshire but found all across England, east of the limestone belt. They are therefore found in the clay and chalk parts of Wiltshire.

Double-aisled plans were being built in the county quite commonly until the late 18th century and there is even an example from about 1860 at Sutton Veny, built for the Everett family's Greenhill estate.

Some barns had only a single aisle. Edward Peters has suggested this was a practice which began in the 17th century. The barn on staddle stones at East Chisenbury, Enford and the L-shaped barn at Cholderton were both single-aisled. There is a late example of a single aisled barn, dated 1818 on the tiebeam, at Pewsey Hill Farm, Pewsey.

Medieval barns

ABOUT 36 WILTSHIRE barns from before 1500 are known though in nine cases only through records as they no longer exist. They are renowned for their superb carpentry. Their distribution is quite widespread with a concentration in the north-west quarter of the county where early timber walls were rebuilt in stone from the 15th century onwards. Most of those lost were in the north-east quarter of the county where there has been urban development, rail and motorway access and pressure to convert farm buildings to other uses.

Known barns from before 1500, the asterisked barns have gone with the date of demolition in brackets.

Location	bays	cruck/aisled	probable builder	date
Aldbourne, Glebe Farm* (c1968)	7?	c	Amesbury Priory	
Atworth, Church Farm	7	c	Shaftesbury Abbey	1326
Atworth, Gt Chalfield		c	Percy family	1340-65
Avebury, Manor Farm	9	c,a	Avebury Priory	1279-1301
Biddestone, Slaughterford	7	c	Monkton Farleigh Priory	
Box, Rudloe Manor	5	c	Monkton Farleigh Priory	1410/30
Bradford-on-Avon, Barton Farm	5	c	Shaftesbury Abbey	1290-1325
Bradford-on-Avon, Barton Farm	14	c	Shaftesbury Abbey	1334-1379
Bradford-on-Avon, Maplecroft	5	c	Besill family	
Bremhill, Field Farm	3	c		1484-5
Bremhill, Manor			Malmesbury Abbey	
Brokenborough	10	c	Malmesbury Abbey	
Burbage, Wulf Hall*(1930+)	7	c	Esturmy family?	
Castle Combe, Hans Farm	4?	c		
Cherhill, Manor Farm*(1956)	9	c,a	Earl of Warwick	
Cricklade, St. Sampson's*(1964)	7	c		
Chilmark*(1826)	9?		Wilton Abbey	
Crudwell	8	c	Malmesbury Abbey	
East Knoyle, Rectory*(early 20 cen?)				
East Knoyle, Upper Leigh Farm	5	c		
Great Somerford	4	c		
Highworth, Manor House*(1910-15)	7	c		
Highworth, Sevenhampton*	7			
Kingston Deverill	7	c,a		1407-1410
Lacock, Manor Farm	9	c	Lacock Abbey	1338-9
Lacock, Wick Farm	5	c?	Croke family	
Longbridge Deverill, Hill Deverill	5			
Lyneham, Bradenstoke*(1929)	9	c?	Bradenstoke Abbey	
Marlborough, Barton Farm*(fire 1976)	5	a	Crown	mid13th C?
Melksham	7	c	Salisbury Dean & Chapter	
Odstock				
Ogbourne St. George, Hallam Farm	7	c	Abbey of Bec?	
Purton	13		Malmesbury Abbey ??	
Steeple Langford, Bathampton Farm	7	c		
Tisbury, Place Farm	13	c	Shaftesbury Abbey	1289-1314

Four barns are usually open to visit; at Avebury and Lacock (both National Trust), Bradford-on-Avon (Historic England, in the care of the Bradford-on-Avon Preservation Trust) and Tisbury (leased by a gallery).

Tree-ring dating has shown that the earliest surviving Wiltshire barns date from the 13th century and the first 30 years of the 14th century. They were built by a variety of ecclesiastical owners and a smaller number of wealthy lay lords. Most of the medieval barns had an odd number of bays. Those with the most bays were the principal barns of the monasteries.

Most of the early barns are or were of cruck construction. There is a record of 1270/71 of a barn of five pairs of forks and a porch at Patney. It belonged to St Swithin's Priory, Winchester.[1] There is a building account for the construction of a barn at Sevenhampton, Highworth in 1280 (Wiltshire Record Society vol. 14). It was probably seven bays long as the account starts with eight trees (or trunks) for the main trusses bought from Braden Forest. It seems to have had a stone-tiled or perhaps shingle roof as 4 shillings was paid for moss to be put in the crevices. This was a common practice at the time. The total cost of building the barn was about £25.

Some aisled barns were also early. A late 13th or early 14th century aisled barn, 110 feet long, at Manor Farm, Cherhill, demolished in 1956, was described by Stuart Rigold in *Wiltshire Archaeological Magazine,* vol. 52. This barn was eight bays long, probably nine originally, and had an aisle on each side. It had two threshing bays with porches on both sides of the building. The walls were initially of vertical planks and the roof, originally thatched, was hipped with gablets.

Cherhill barn from a sketch by E. Eades and a section.

Two aisled barns with interesting features were at Barton Farm, Marlborough (just outside the outer bailey of Marlborough Castle) and at Avebury. The Marlborough barn had chamfered and roll stopped aisle posts. The Great Barn at Avebury, open to the public, was rebuilt, again with aisles, in the late 17th century but retains two end crucks, an early feature, tree-ring dated to1275-1311. It was part of the home farm of Avebury Manor, the former site of a Benedictine cell. The still existing barn at Manor Farm, Kingston Deverill, aisled with base crucks like Cherhill, has been tree-ring dated to about 1407-10. A building account for 1407-8 shows that the reeve travelled to find workmen from far and wide to build it.

The earliest existing barn without aisles is at Place Farm, Tisbury. It dates from 1289-1314 and has cruck trusses. It originally had one threshing bay in its 13 bay length. Lesser doorways were added later and one end was then converted to accommodation. It belonged to Shaftesbury Abbey.

*South barn at Barton Farm, Marlborough,
the large chamfered aisle post and moulded
foot, 1965. The barn was repaired in the
early 18th century.*

The barn at Church Farm, Atworth, dendro-dated to 1326, also belonged to Shaftesbury. This had one end converted to accommodation in 1588-1613 and the other end was floored over to make a stall.

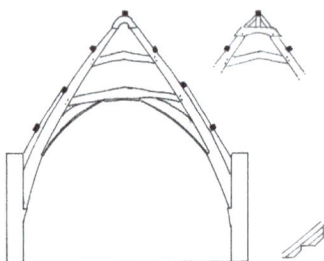

Great barn at Place Farm, Tisbury.

*Converted end of great barn at Church Farm, Atworth, dendro-dated 1326 with the
conversion c.1588-1613. The far end was made into stalls.*

After the medieval period changes in agriculture with less arable meant that many of the largest barns had at least part converted to another use. By 1538 the barn at Melksham was divided, with half still used as a barn and half to house cattle. The barn at Lacock dated 1338-9 also eventually proved too large and one end was converted into a market hall, probably in the 18th century. The demolished aisled barn at Highworth is pictured in the early 20th century lined with cattle stalls. Glebe Farm barn at Aldbourne was similarly equipped.

Cruck barn at Glebe Farm, Aldbourne with added accommodation for cattle (Source: Historic England Archive).

Crucks were still in use for barn construction in the county until the end of the 15th century. The small barn at Bremhill dated 1484-5 survived, when recorded, in a state of near completeness. The trusses were earth-fast (set into the ground). The barn at Great Somerford was recorded with the trusses on sill beams set on rubble sleeper walls. It is likely that all the county's cruck barns originally had full height crucks on sill beams or dwarf walls. In the stone areas walls were progressively heightened over time to eaves level. Even at Bradford-on-Avon where the walls of the great barn are of one build there is some evidence that they result from a major rebuilding when sloping ground caused the structure to start to fail. The proof that a stone barn was formerly timber-framed is the presence of a cruck spur, the small timber which joined the cruck blade to a wall post. If it has gone there may still be a pair of pegholes in the cruck at eaves level.

A characteristic of early barns is to have steep, narrow windbraces. Also the purlins are scarfed at the trusses. When built in stone the barns have buttresses at each roof truss position and often also at the ends. Most of the early barns were thatched but many became tiled at a later date.

Hallam Farm barn, Ogbourne St. George, showing a cruck spur to a wall post.

above: Original plinth and later walling above and cruck truss 4 and cruck spur, Church Farm, Atworth.

left: Steep, thin windbraces and diagonal scarf joint at the truss, Church Farm, Atworth.

16th and 17th century barns

THERE ARE A few surviving 16th century barns. It was the end of the monastic period and most monasteries had already provided their estates with excellent quality buildings. 16th and 17th century stone and timber barns tend to follow the local medieval practice of having plain gabled ends to the main roof and the porch roofs. Examples are the barns at Box Manor, Westwood Manor and at Crudwell. Those which have been identified and recorded, most commonly had roof trusses with a tiebeam, collar and vertical or raking (sloping) queen struts.

The barn at Spencer's Farm in the centre of Wroughton is an example of the complicated history of many barns. It originated as a 17th century 3-bay timber-framed structure on low sarsen walls. The western part was rebuilt in the 18th century as a single aisled section. The east end was rebuilt, possibly in the late 18th century, providing accommodation for cattle or implements. Finally a sarsen-walled extension at the west end, probably in the early 19th century, provided a stable and tackroom. Plans for community use came to nothing and there was an application for demolition in 1995.

above: Barn at Crudwell.
below: Five-bay barn of c. 1500 at Westwood Manor, Westwood. The end bay, right, near the road was probably used to store hay for the adjoining oxhouse.

above left: Barn at Spencer's Farm, Wootton Bassett. above right: 17th century barn at Manor Farm, Stockton. left: Wall brace (at the above), using possibly part of a cruck from an earlier building and sill beam with an old mortice at left end.

Position in the farmstead

WITHIN THE FARMSTEAD the barn may be found in a variety of positions but in Wiltshire it is quite commonly end on to the road. If the house faces south to the road or has its back to the road, the barn then runs north/south forming a yard between itself and the house. The prevailing wind will then be blowing west/east through the threshing bay helping to winnow the corn. A few examples from different periods of this positioning are at the Manor House, Box, Lower Easton Farm, Corsham and Pound Farm, Bromham. Barns running east/west can be found, for example, at Barton Farm, Bradford-on-Avon (where an earlier barn runs north/south) and at Rudloe Manor, Box.

Barns were often attached to farmhouses in the upland Pennine area of England and such a building was called a laithe house. A similar practice is found in the limestone area of north-west Wiltshire where the buildings usually date from the 18th century. Examples have been recorded in the parishes of Winsley, Corsham, Box, Yatton Keynell, Hullavington and Grittleton. In 1749 an interlinked farmhouse and barn were built at Webbs Farm, Chiseldon but here the barn is at right-angles to the end of the farmhouse. In most cases the two are in line. In one case at Easton, Corsham the 18th century barn forms the tail of a T behind a medieval farmhouse.

Plan types

E DWARD PETERS CLASSIFIED British barn plans into five types. Type 1 is a symmetrical building with a central threshing floor. Type 2 is a symmetrical building with two threshing floors. Type 3 has a single threshing floor placed off-centre. Type 4 has a threshing floor across the end of the barn. The final type, 5, has part of the storage bays set at a higher level than the threshing floor. The space below is used for another purpose; as a cowshed, a stable or a cartshed so the barn has become a 'combination' building.

left: Type 1 barn at Little Ashley Farm, Winsley. The hipped porch has wide-planked doors with integral buildings each side. There are also buildings attached to the end walls. right: Type 2 barn at the home farm of Chilton House, Chilton Foliat. The 11 bays are partitioned into 2 parts. It is timber-framed on a brick plinth which has the date 1773 set in it. The kingpost roof is covered with plain tiles.

left: Type 3 barn at Park Farm, Westrop, Corsham. right: Early 19th century type 4 barn at East Farm, Atworth. Next to the porch is an added pigsty.

left: Type 5, Chaldicotts Farm, Semley, a barn with a lofted stable at the far end. right: Mid-19th century type 5 barn at Pound Farm, Bromham. The barn is 4 bays long with provision for cattle facing the threshing bay in the long end, the cart-horse stable to the right in 3 bays long. It has a bolted kingpost roof.

The type 3 barns are thought to have been used for storing threshed straw at the short end and unthreshed corn in the longer end. Jeremy Lake has said that they are particularly common in upland areas for oats and were also more popular after the introduction of threshing machines in the 1780s. It is also possible that livestock were accommodated at the 'long' end. This was a very common practice in the county which is clearly shown in the structure of the type 5 barns but may have left very little evidence when there was no loft over the animals. They were usually tethered facing along the axis of the building with their heads towards the threshing bay. Keeping animals in part of the barn was an old practice. The farm buildings mentioned in documents include the 1649 Swallowcliffe 'barn and stable' and the 1671 Trowbridge 'barn and stall' and 'barn and stable'. The stable with the 17th century barn at East Farm, Preston, Lyneham was added later.

Preston East Farm, Lyneham. Early 17th century timber-framed barn. Beyond the original timber end wall is an added stone stable with a loft above.

When another building with a pent roof was built backing on to the end of the barn, the old term for this was a 'cut end' or 'cutting'. Bromham Rectory in 1608 had a barn of five fields and 'a cut end thereunto adjoining for a stable'.

Type 4 barns with the threshing bay at the end are not common in the county. It is thought that only the threshed straw was stored in such barns and the corn was in ricks. In 1631 a copyholder at Dinton had 'a barn of 1 room and a threshing floor'. Other barns of this type have been found at Kington St Michael, Yatton Keynell and Corsham.

All five types of barn are found in Wiltshire and there are also several regional types; the barn with a covered cartway through it and the L-shaped barn. These occur in the 'lowland' area of Wiltshire, the area of principally timber building to the east and south of the limestone belt.

The covered cartway, unlike a threshing bay, has a solid partition on each side. An

L-shaped barn may be quite large and incorporate a cartway. At Lower Bridmore Farm, Berwick St. John one arm of the barn is dated 1772 and the other 1781.

Cartway between the two barns at Manor Farm, Chitterne.

Roofs and porches

BARNS FROM THE 18th and early 19th centuries often have half-hipped roofs, indicating that they were once thatched if no longer so. At Ganbrook Farm, Atworth only the porch roof is half-hipped.

Barn at Ganbrook Farm, Atworth in 1982. The barn, formerly thatched, has a central porch and through way for loaded waggons. It is in a yard which originated as an isolated field barn complex in existence by 1773. Within the yard were a barn, stable and cowshed. Note the remaining side wall of a lean-to.

In the second half of the 18th century and especially around 1800 and the early 19th century, the full hip became more fashionable. Catslide roofs, continuing the slope of the main barn roof, were also used around 1800. One example is the barn of 1817 at Green Farm, Nettleton.

Barn at Elm House Farm, Biddestone.

Windbraces, strengthening the roof along its length, were widely used in Wiltshire houses until the 16th century when rooms were often open to the roof but they were less used domestically after this because upper floors gave the building more rigidity. However, in barns, which were open from floor to rafters, windbraces remained vital. They are therefore still found in barns of the 18th century but straight rather than curved and perhaps on only one side of the truss. They continued in the form of long diagonal braces bisecting the rafters as long as large barns were built.

Wall features

THE PLINTH WALLS supporting the framing of timber barns were of local materials. 16th and 17th century barns usually have a stone plinth. The barn at Great Wishford has an 18th century plinth of mixed materials. 18th and 19th century plinths in many areas were of brick and the size and appearance of the bricks often helps with dating.

The timber wall above the plinth can often be dated by the type of bracing in the wall and type of jowled post. 16th and 17th century wall braces were usually curved. 18th and 19th century braces are straighter and often bisect other timbers in the wall.

Timber barns usually have a cladding of weather boards on the outside. The space between the boards provides some light and ventilation though there may also be some timber windows.

Stone barns, however, need more ventilation. Ventilation slits, also called lancet windows, are often presumed to indicate an early date for a barn but they occur at all periods with slight variations. Unusually at the medieval barn, Church Farm, Atworth, they are triangular but they are in added walling of perhaps 15th or 16th century date. Late 18th or 19th century examples in some areas have brick dressings.

left: Wall bracing at Home Farm, Roundway. right: North barn, Barton Farm, Marlborough with wide plank weatherboarding in the end wall.

left: Triangular vent lined with timber in the added stone walls, Church Farm, Atworth.
centre: Stone window, Trimnells Farm barn, Colerne.
right: Lancet windows and putlog holes for scaffolding, Place Farm, Tisbury.

Dove lofts and owl holes

PROVISION FOR PIGEONS was often made in the barns of the limestone area of Wiltshire either in the end walls, the porches or occasionally along a side wall. This is an old custom which is referred to above in the Sherston reference of 1649. One of the oldest examples recorded is at Manor Farm, Yatton Keynell but the tradition continued as long as traditional barns were being built. There was a strong preference for a tiered triangular pattern of holes. Inside the barn the doveloft was in either part or all of the porch roof. The door to it was reached by ladder.

Owl holes have been claimed as an innovation of the 1720s but there is ample evidence in Wiltshire of their use before this date. The upper opening at Yatton Keynell appears to be one and there are similar openings in some medieval barns. The barn at New Farm, Lacock has an owl nesting box, probably dating from the 19th century, attached to a roof truss. Owl holes are also found on stables where the owls would have been equally useful in keeping down vermin.

left: Pigeon loft and owl hole above the porch in the mid-17th century barn at Manor Farm, Yatton Keynell.
right: Door into the pigeon loft, Pinkney Court Farm, Sherston.

Doors

Not all barns have porches. When there are no porches there is usually either a large door, a low door (for an unloaded waggon) or a pedestrian door opposite. If there is only a small door at the other side the practice was not to pull the loaded waggon through the barn but to back it in for unloading. The pedestrian door was used to create a draught during winnowing. This was the process after threshing when the grain was thrown up for the chaff to be blown away. In the occasional examples of barns without a door opposite the entrance, it is likely that the winnowing took place outside.

The doors are usually of planks, usually the wider the older they are. Barn doors have very often been renewed since the barn was built. There may be a bolt hole in the jamb for the door to be barricaded. There may also have been a low structure called a lift, used during winnowing to retain the grain.

The threshing floor

Wiltshire is fortunate in its many literary descriptions of threshing. Stephen Duck the 'thresher poet' born in 1705 at Charlton near Upavon is often quoted. Wiltshire Museum has part of a tiebeam with a carving of a flail threshing scene dated 1788 which came from a barn on the outskirts of the town. A. G. Street described winnowing by machine at Ditchampton Farm, Wilton. One man turned the handle, one filled the machine with grain using a huge scoop shovel, one minded the sacks of cleaned corn and a fourth weighed off and tallied.

Davis says that in South Wiltshire the threshing floor was usually of oak planks two inches thick laid on oak sleepers. To prevent rats and mice burrowing underneath they were often laid on a bed of flints or cinders or sometimes they rested on brick piers fifteen or eighteen inches high so that dogs and cats could pass under them. Air space below also prevented the floor from rotting. He says that each threshing floor either within one barn or in several barns was used for a different type of grain. In the 20th century many threshing floors were replaced by concrete.

left: Lift at Manor Farm, Chitterne.
right: Slot for lift at Lower Easton Farm, Corsham.

left: Stone base for plank threshing floor, Barton Farm, Bradford-on-Avon.
right: Threshing floor, Place Farm, Tisbury.

In the porch or side wall near the threshing floor there is often an alcove, probably for a lamp to use at night when stock were kept in the barn or for tools. Stone porches may have a pedestrian entrance door. Tally marks made by the farm workers are often found in this area and other doodles and graffiti. Dated initials are frequently seen. They may not give a construction date for the barn but they indicate when it was already in existence. A number of Wiltshire barns are more formally dated by an inscription on a tiebeam, wall post, quoin or plinth, usually facing on to the threshing bay.

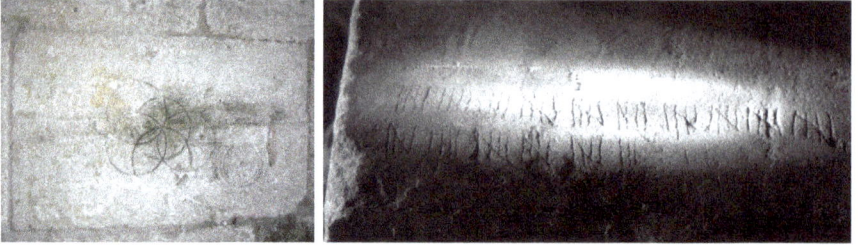

left: Various superstitious graffiti in the porch at Barton Farm, Bradford-on-Avon.
right: Tally marks at Lower Easton Farm, Corsham.

Attached buildings

WILTSHIRE BARNS WERE often constructed with lean-to buildings in the angles next to the porches or buildings were added in that position at a later date. Sometimes only the side wall of an added building remains. These added buildings were often loose boxes for calves, implement sheds or pigsties.

Truss for lean-to building to barn, Rodmead Farm, Maiden Bradley.

Staddle barns

ANOTHER REGIONAL TYPE is the barn on staddle stones which first appeared in the late 18th century. It is somewhat similar to a granary in appearance but is a great deal larger. It should perhaps be seen as just an enclosed version of the rick in the yard which was also built on staddle stones. The Wiltshire name for the platform was a 'rick staffel' or 'stavel' — stavel being an old Germanic word for a support or prop. Davis uses the term 'stavel barn' and says they were used for wheat.

Peter Nicholson found that many have shallow porch-like structures on one side of the threshing floor and all have the typical opposing doors each side, often of stable door type, split horizontally so the upper part can be opened to allow a through draught to carry the dust and husks away.

Barns on staddle stones have been recorded, for example, in the Clyffe Pypard area (Grigson mentions one gone by 1948), at Potterne, at East Chisenbury, Enford (this one now removed to Bristol), at Countess Farm, Amesbury, dated 1772, at the Home Farm of Clarendon Park and at Conholt Park, Chute. At Countess Farm there are both a granary and a staddle barn. There, the framework of the barn stands on nine staddle stones along and four across, the granary on four by three. The barn also has opposed central doorways and the granary a single door.

The barn at Priory Farm, Burcombe Without was one of two 'stavil barns' mentioned in 1793 and extensive repairs were recorded in 1864. It had a granary at one end and a loose box for a cow at the other, probably entered with a ramp. It was originally thatched with tiles replacing between 1905 and 1920.

Staddle barn at Home Farm, Clarendon Park.

Staddle barn at Priory Farm, Burcombe Without, there by 1793 and extensively repaired in 1864.

Priory Farm, Burcombe left: Side to the road, with end door to loose box.
right: Interior looking to the granary.

Mill barns and machinery

I N THE 19TH century there were several new sources of power for operating early threshing and other machinery; horse wheel houses and stationary or portable steam engines. In the wheel houses the horses walked round circular platforms, usually inside a circular or angular building attached to the barn, operating a gearing mechanism. Animal power was not a new idea in itself. Most earlier forms had involved treadmills though there had been horse-powered cider mills since the mid-17th century. A number of examples of horse engines attached to barns have been found in Wiltshire. Good examples have been seen at Park Farm, Chilton Foliat and Manor Farm, Steeple Ashton. They are thought to have originated around 1800 and to have been in use during most of the 19th century. Often very little remains to show where they stood. At New Farm, Lacock only sections of curved wall on the barn porch and side wall mark where a horse wheel stood. At Barton Farm, Bradford-on-Avon the stone platform remains, along with some mutilation of the buttresses and evidence of a hole made in the wall for transmission of power to the barn interior. At Roundway Farm, Roundway the building

Horse gin house attached to a 5-bay, 18th century aisled barn at Park Farm, Chilton
Foliat. The gin house has vertical timber cladding and dates from the 19th century.

left: Horse mill at Manor Farm, Steeple Ashton.
right: Interior at Manor Farm showing some protective boarding remaining.

was converted into a garage losing its shaped front wall but features surviving include rails on one side to protect the building from the working horse.

Occasionally a stream was used to power machinery through a mill wheel. A good example is at Little Chalfield, Atworth. An earlier water mill there was replaced by a very tall barn into which the power was brought from an iron millwheel to drive machinery. Sale particulars of 1888 explained the height of the barn as suitable for the housing of elevators etc. In the early 20th century two low rooms were constructed in brickwork at the west end of the barn and the drive from the mill was conducted to them to power several processes. In one of the rooms there was a Coventry Climax water pump probably dating from the 1920s. So the power of the mill stream was used to drive a pump to send water from the stream round the farm. This was a very neat labour-saving idea.

Mill barn at Little Chalfield, Atworth.

Field barns

I N CONTRAST TO the usual close association of house and barn, there are also many examples in Wiltshire of field barns or yards. These are chiefly found in isolated positions on higher ground, on the limestone hills in the northwest of the county, for example at Nettleton and Malmesbury Without and on the chalk downs of Salisbury Plain and the Marlborough area. They were used to store fodder close to the animals and, when the unit included a yard and cowsheds, to produce manure where it could easily be applied to the fields. Sometimes the unit included a farm cottage which sometimes developed into a separate farm. This was the case at Ganbrook Farm, Atworth.

There were already a few field barns in the 17th century and many more are marked on Andrews and Dury's map of 1773. Davis speaks of its not being uncommon in South Wiltshire for great farms to have field barns due to the elongated shape of many parishes. He says they were not usually used for wheat, which was valuable, but for barley and oats.

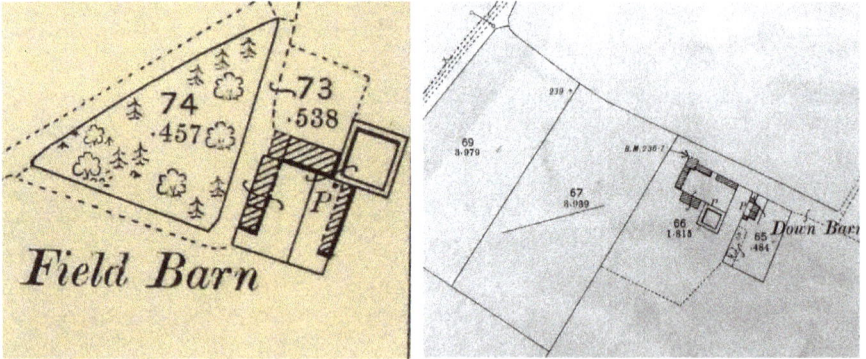

left: Field barn of Netherhampton Farm in 1901.
right: A field barn with cottages in 1926.

Barn of the field barn, Netherhampton Farm, built between 1854 and 1889, with sliding double doors to the threshing bay and a sliding taking-in door.

Part of the field barn of a Salisbury Plain farm.

Polebarns, hay houses and fodder houses

THERE IS A Polebarn Road in Trowbridge and the barn's outline is shown on a late 18th century map. Hay houses and fodder houses are mentioned in documents. It is likely that as a separate building they were simply a roof on posts or pillars. A copyholder at Stanton St Bernard in 1631 had 'a hay house lately built upon posts'. Sometimes a hay house reference seems to imply a loft over a stable or cowhouse or an attached lean-to.

Dutch barns

THESE METAL FRAMED barns, mainly for hay, were first introduced in the 1880s and many were built just after World War I. Some have quite decorative ironwork.

left: Dutch barn, Lower Easton Farm, Corsham.
right: Dutch barn by the same maker, Manor Farm, Erlestoke.

Interior of the Dutch barn, Dudmore Lodge Farm, Aldbourne.

Malting barns and wool lofts

THESE TWO BARN-LIKE types of building are occasionally found on Wiltshire farms and should not be confused with ordinary agricultural barns.

Most **malthouses** were separate establishments in towns or villages, sometimes adjoining a public house or brewery. Malting was a major industry in the county. However, in some cases they were part of a working farm, either attached to the farmhouse as at Malthouse, Wilsford, Poplar Farm, Atworth and Westcourt Farm, Burbage or separate as at Home Farm, Biddestone. A malting barn was on two levels. Barley arrived on the lower floor and was put into a steeping tank. This might be carved out of solid stone, the old name was a 'yoting stone' or made from ashlar stones finely jointed together. After this the wet barley was spread on the floor to germinate. It was then put on the floor over the malt kiln at the end of the building spread on perforated tiles. Before the 18th century the tiles were made of stone but later they were ceramic, 1 foot square and 2 inches thick (3cm by .5cm). Those at Biddestone rested on iron bars about four feet (1.22m) above the furnace and under the floor a deflector plate was set on stone pillars. Kilning stopped the germination. The grains were then spread out on the upper floor again and turned regularly. Finally, they were milled and the malt was bagged.

The malthouse at Wilsford was timber-framed with the kiln end attached to the farmhouse. There are references to malting equipment in the 17th century inventories and there were 13 bushels of malt there in 1615. The barn walls were infilled in brick as a repair in 1770. The upper floor was of planks covered with gypsum. Some of the original stone malting tiles were re-used in a partition. The square vent above the kiln was made of planks.

Malting barn at the Malthouse, Wilsford. The kiln is at the far end attached to the farmhouse.

Malt stones re-used as a partition. The boarded vent from below and in the roof.
[Also Wilsford]

The Biddestone maltings seem to have started in the late 18th century and were enlarged in the 19th century. Work stopped after July 1914, the date of a newspaper found in the furnace.

left: The malthouse complex at Home Farm, Biddestone. The stair leads to a granary.
centre: Steeping tank of ashlar stone.
right: Stoke hole of the kiln.

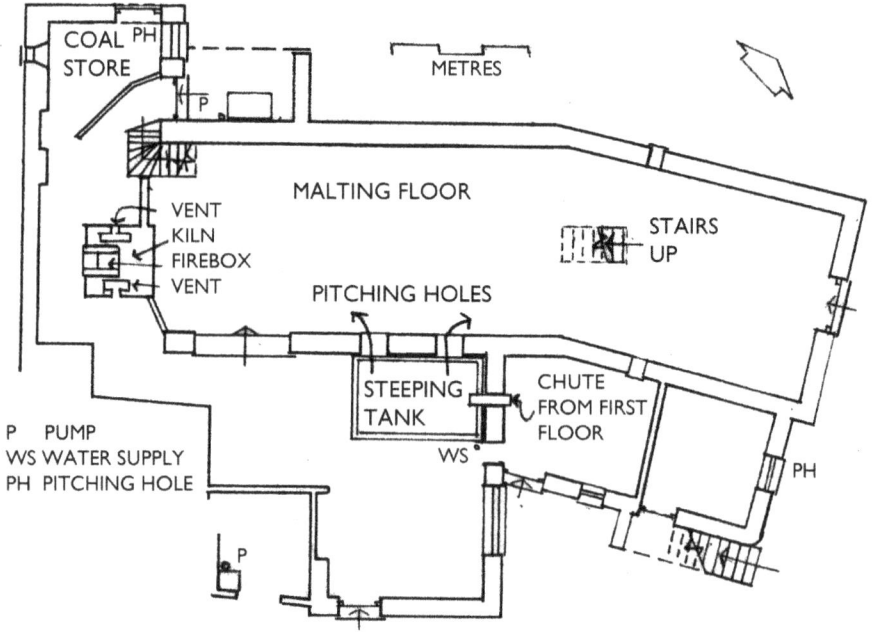

COAL PH
STORE
P

METRES

MALTING FLOOR

VENT
KILN
FIREBOX
VENT

PITCHING HOLES

STAIRS
UP

STEEPING
TANK

CHUTE
FROM FIRST
FLOOR

WS

P   PUMP
WS WATER SUPPLY
PH PITCHING HOLE

P

PH

Home Farm, Biddestone, ground floor plan.

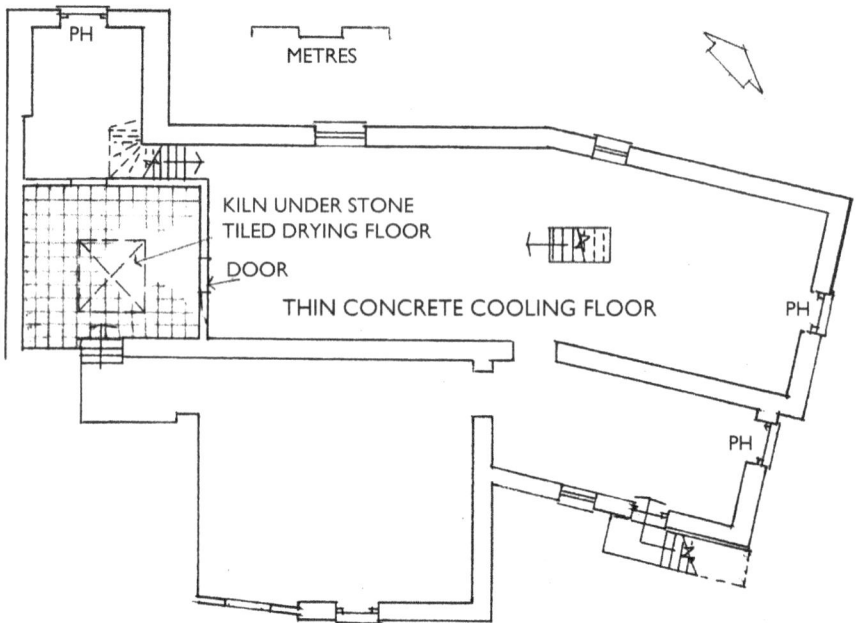

PH

METRES

KILN UNDER STONE
TILED DRYING FLOOR

DOOR

THIN CONCRETE COOLING FLOOR

PH

PH

Home Farm, Biddestone, first floor plan.

left: Half-arch by the kiln.   centre: Stone stair to the first floor.
right: The malting floor looking towards the kiln.

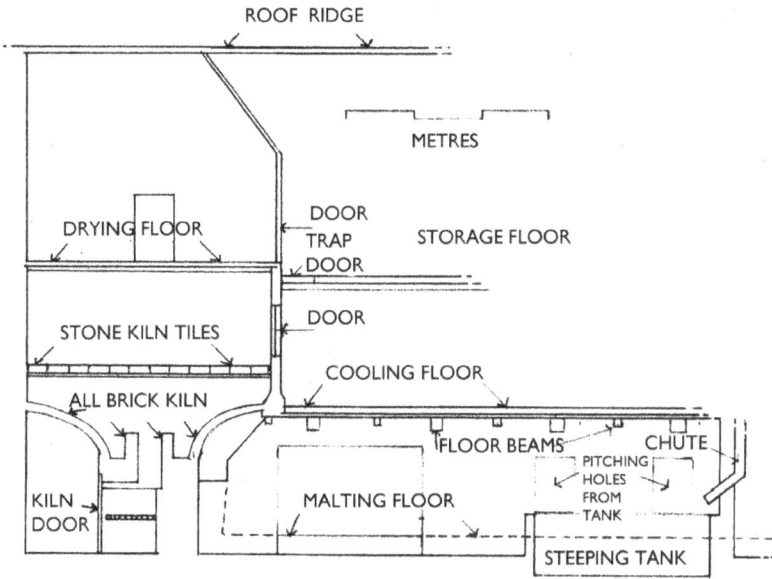

Home Farm, Biddestone, section.

Some stone malting tiles were smaller than those at Wilsford and perhaps dated from the 18th century rather than earlier. There is also some variation in the brick tiles but they became fairly standardised in the 19th century.

Malt stone set in the wall, Poplar Farm, Atworth.

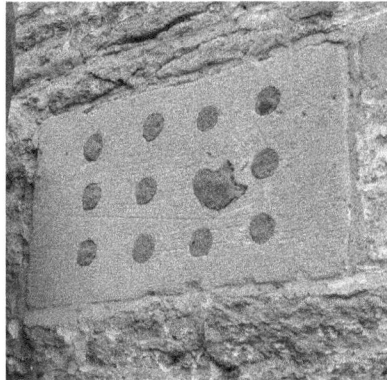

left: Drain made from a malting tile? Roundway Farm, Roundway.
centre and right: 19th century malting tile; large holes on the underside leading to a
cluster of small holes above.

Wool lofts were the warehouses where clothiers stored wool or processed cloth. Documents show that they were quite common in parts of the county. Though also floored over, the main distinguishing features from malting barns are that they were smaller, had more partitioning and, of course, did not include a kiln. The 15th century Priory Barn at Bradford-on-Avon was floored and was probably a wool loft or perhaps a warehouse for furs and meat from the large rabbit warren on the hillside above. It has contemporary living accommodation at one end. The building of 1575–80 used as the Fox Talbot Museum at Lacock includes a lodge at one end, a stair at the rear and a taking-in doorway at the front. It was also possibly a wool loft.

Granaries

T HE GRANARY WAS the store for the vital seed corn kept for planting the following year. The grain had to be secure from both human and animal predators and kept in the best possible conditions. In Wiltshire it was often called the garner or gardiner. Originally many farmers may have kept the seed corn within the farmhouse. This tradition probably continued at least into the 18th century on some farms in the limestone area of north-west Wiltshire where the ample roof spaces reached by stairs were suitable for all kinds of storage. Occasionally grain is still found where it has trickled under the floorboards.

The oldest granary in the county is at Barton Farm, Bradford-on-Avon. It is cruck-built on tall tapering stone pillars and has been tree-ring dated to between 1370 and 1390. The walls and the lower area have gradually been filled with stone but the timbers are still remarkably complete.

A logical progression for security was to construct the granary attached to or close to the farmhouse. It is difficult to establish how many farms before 1700 had

Barton Farm, Bradford-on-Avon. There were formerly also steps from the other direction.

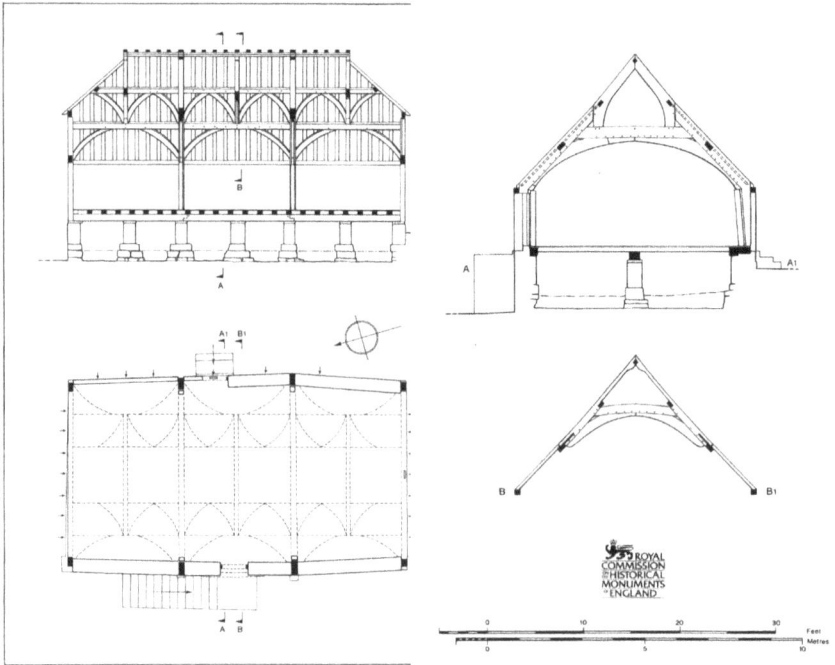

Barton Farm, Bradford-on-Avon (© Crown Copyright. Historic England Archive)

separate granaries. Documentary sources only rarely mention them, particularly in the lowland areas of the county. In the 18th century they became much more common.

Sometimes, the granary was situated over another farm building and reached by an outside stair. The most common position found in many parts of Europe was over a cartshed. There is an example with tapered stone pillars at West Sevington Farm, Grittleton and one over a waggon shed at Manor Farm, West Yatton, Yatton Keynell. Other positions quoted earlier in this book include a 'cornhouse and whitehouse (dairy)' at Bradford-on-Avon in 1695 and, in the 18th century, a granary over a

left: Stone granary at Coles Farm, Box, originally detached but now with a linking section to the farmhouse of 1641.
right: Brick granary of 1718 close to the farmhouse at Manor Farm, Semington.

left: Granary above the cart shed, West Sevington Farm, Grittleton.
right: Granary in the loft of a waggon shed at Manor Farm, West Yatton, Yatton Keynell.

brewhouse was built at the end of the service range attached to the farmhouse at New Farm, Lacock. Another common position, quoted earlier in this book, was in the loft over a stable with access by a stone stair.

The structure of the granaries

M OST SURVIVING GRANARIES are timber-framed, probably because timber was the preferred material to be in contact with the grain. Timber granaries were still being constructed in north-west Wiltshire in the 18th century when all other buildings were of stone. Frequently the structural timbers are protected by an outer layer of weatherboarding. This is not always the case. At A'Becketts, West Lavington there was a timber granary with original brick infilling in which the timbers had always been uncovered. Second to timber, brick seems to have been preferred. At Rodmead Farm, Maiden Bradley the brick is in English Garden Wall bond, suggesting an early 19th century date. It appears to have been white-washed like the brick example (above) of 1718 at Semington.

left: Timber-framed granary with original brick infilling associated with a house of 1767. A'Becketts, Littleton Panell, West Lavington. The corner post has a flared , type C, jowl.
right: Brick granary at Rodmead Farm, Maiden Bradley.

There is some variation in size between granaries. Where more storage space was required on largely arable farms, the building was sometimes two storeys high.

left: Two-storey granaries: Samways, Alvediston.
right: Littlecote Park Farm, Chilton Foliat.

Most granaries of timber or brick were constructed on staddle stones which were set in lines under the building. This was often in rows, three by three or four by three. This was to protect the contents from rats and mice. Consequently the steps outside were usually moveable but permanent steps have sometimes been built later for convenience. An additional protection from vermin was to allow the farm cats entry and there is very often a cat hole in the door. Owls could be encouraged in by leaving a small window in the gable unglazed.

The staddle stones vary considerably in design. Those shown at Alvediston have a taller cap than those shown at Semington. Peter Nicholson pointed out that the base or column can be square or round, tapering from some 20" (.5m) wide at ground level to 8"-10" (.2-.25m) wide at the top. The height of the column can vary from under 2' (.6m) to well over 4' (1.22m). At Fussell's Lodge Farm, Clarendon Park the base was square, tapering, with the corners slightly chamfered. The capstones may be as large as two feet in diameter with the shaping varying from a flat cheese with a vertical edge, to rounded coming to a fine edge, with many having a heavy chamfer on their upper face

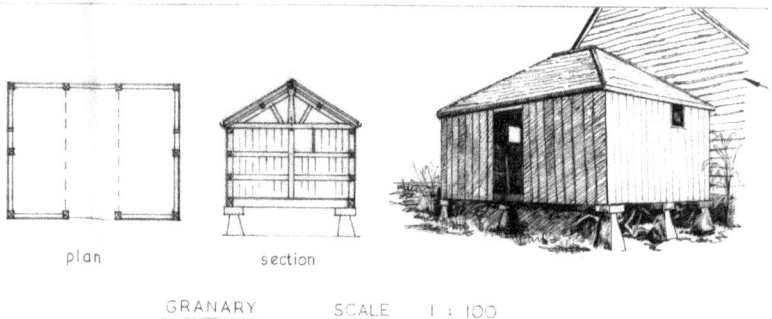

plan   section

GRANARY   SCALE   I : 100

Three bay granary at Chilton House, Chilton Foliat (drawing Peter C. Jackson 1984).

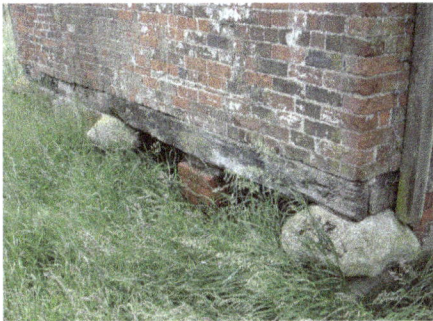

Staddle stones: Forest Farm, Melksham and Rodmead Farm, Maiden Bradley.

leaving a flat area about the same size as the top of the base. One at Nonsuch Farm, Clyffe Pypard has initials carved in it and another at Notton, Lacock has an egg and dart decoration around the top edge.

An alternative to staddle stones was to build the structure on brick piers. It is sometimes said that the tunnels between were used to house poultry or, if they were larger, pigs but it is uncertain if they were designed for this purpose. There are three granaries on brick piers with segmental arches at Purton. One at the Manor House with a dovecote in the upper storey is dated 1746, another of two storeys at College Farm is dated 1754 and the third at South Pavenhill Farm is dated 1765. A late 19th century example on brick arches is at Rudloe Manor, Box.

Granary of 1810 on brick piers with a dove loft above, Tytherington Farm, Sutton Veny.

Fittings

THERE WAS A need to keep the interior clean and dry. In timber granaries this was often achieved by a lining of planks around the walls. In a stone-built upper floor granary at Little Chalfield the walls were lined with interlocking blocks of ashlar stone. The grain might be stored in sacks or in boarded grain bins. A ladder or stair led to the upper floor in a two storey granary.

The roofs of granaries are small and often simply constructed. They were most frequently thatched and if the thatch has been replaced, there is often a half-hip at each end of the roof. In the early 19th century they were often fully hipped. A number of taller granaries have sling brace roof trusses to keep the loft clear.

Granaries are also found at malthouses, and were used to store either the unprocessed barley grains or sacks of the finished malt. In 1561 Richard Brent of

left: Interior stone wall of the granary at Little Chalfield Farm, Atworth.
right: Boarded wall at Fussells Lodge Farm, Clarendon Park.

Granary bins, Ugford Farm, Burcombe Without.
Chain hoist in the granary at Upper Combe Farm, Castle Combe.

Warminster had a 'gardiner' containing 7 quarters of malt. At Home Farm, Biddestone, outside steps lead up to the granary attached to the malthouse (page 49).

Granaries were still being built in very much the traditional way in the 19th century. Only details of the carpentry indicate the date. A newspaper report of January 1861 illustrates both the use of the granary and the importance still of security when times were harsh. A man was prosecuted for the theft of a sack and two bushels of beans from the locked granary of his master at Pewsey. They were taken from a bin where beans were mixed with black oats. The weather was so wet that the labouring poor could not work. There was 'deep distress' and many thefts of food.

Stables

IT SEEMS LIKELY that few horses were kept on ordinary Wiltshire farms in the medieval period. Oxen were used for ploughing and hauling, and horses would have been used only for personal transport and, in trains, as pack animals. It was a requirement for a knight to have a horse and the great lords, who had retinues of followers, needed to provide stabling. Consequently lodging ranges usually had dormitories on the first floor and stabling below. Examples are the 15th century ranges at Brook House Farm, Heywood and at South Wraxall Manor. In the medieval period as horses were few, many stables occupied one end of an oxhouse or barn.

15th century lodging range at Brook House, Heywood with stables on the ground floor and sleeping accommodation above.

From the 16th century onwards there is evidence for the keeping of horses more generally and from 1600 they are mentioned more often in wills and inventories. The increase in the number of horses kept sometimes led to medieval buildings with other functions being converted to stables. The chapel at Sheldon Manor, Chippenham Without was converted in this way.

The stables which survive from the 16th century are prestigious blocks for the topmost levels of Wiltshire society. The 16th century stable range at Westwood Manor has hollow-moulded mullioned windows. A two-storey stone stable block of 16th or early 17th century date at Maddington, Shrewton was drawn and described by Richard Deane and Kirsty Rodwell.[1]

The early references to farm buildings already quoted show that separate stable buildings on parsonage and manor farms were quite common in the 17th century. A few such early detached stables have been recorded though they are often much altered. Most are of stone.

Stables adjoining the house at Ridge Farm, Neston, Corsham.

left: Stable with datestone I H 1649 for John Hancock at Great Lypiatt Farm, Corsham. Formerly thatched and with ovolo moulded windows. A cartshed with granary above was added at an early date at the far end.
right: 17th century stable at Upper Westwood, Westwood. To the right an added 18th century coach house.

A greater number of 18th century stables can be found situated in most parts of the county. Carthorses were now in widespread use. The stables were larger to house the greater number of animals and the animals themselves were larger. They were objects of pride. Large farms vied with each other to send the best looking teams to market.

Nag stable to the left and carthorse stable to the right at Rowden Farm, Lacock. 1750 is marked on a quoin.

left: 18th century stable, Ganbrook Farm, Atworth, the thatch replaced by stone tiles. right: Carthorse stable at Starveall Farm, Chippenham Without. Probably early 18th century.

During the 18th century it was fashionable to build small nag (riding or coach horse) stables in tower form. The upper floor might be a dovecote or accommodate a groom. Some stables were even more 'architectural' in form with elaborate ornamentation. These were always for carriage or riding horses and often incorporated a coach house. There was a practice at the upper end of the scale to have a tiled area above the manger. An example of this is at Tedworth House, Tidworth. These are not true farm buildings. Similarly, stables were built at inns, breweries, and other commercial premises and at chapels and turnpike houses. Racing stables developed in the county in the 19th century, particularly in the downland areas. Those at

Beckhampton, Avebury developed from an inn. It has early gas lighting in the stable grilles and a central reservoir under the yard as a water supply and for fire fighting.

Early 18th century stable with mullion and transom upper window to the groom's accommodation and the corner fireplace there, Belle Cour Farm, Wingfield.

left: Stable of 1810 with matching side rooms (the left one gone) at Tytherington Farm, Sutton Veny.
right: Early 1860s stable at Netherhampton Farm, Netherhampton.

All kinds and combinations of local building materials were used in the construction of stables.

left: Early 19th century stable at Austin's Farm, Compton Bassett in 1982. The walls are of chalk blocks and the thatched roof survives. There is no loft over the stalls.
right: Banded brickwork and flint. Stable at Dudmore Lodge, Aldbourne, not on a 1809 map but shown in 1818.

left: Carthorse stable of squared sarsen blocks with brick dressings, North Farm, West Overton. The stable has the inscribed date 1802. The roof was formerly thatched. Notice the hit-and-miss window, the apron of sarsen cobbles outside and the cart and machinery shed at the end.
right: Brick 19th century stable at Manor Farm, Erlestoke.

Doorways and windows

IN WILTSHIRE THE most usual plan type has the entrance facing the horses' tails and the interior, if a nag stable, is divided into two or three stalls. A few have been recorded with stalls at right angles to the entrance, usually when the stable is part of a combination building, for example when it is part of a barn.

Doorway surrounds were usually plainer than they were in houses of the same date. However, the 16th century stable at Westwood has a chamfered doorway and an 18th century stable at Slaughterford, Biddestone has a doorway with imposts and keystone. A stable doorway was normally wider than a house door and the door itself was split in half so that the top half could be left open and plenty of air could circulate in the stable.

A stable always had at least one window. Stable windows on especially well-built farmsteads might be mullioned or even mullioned and transomed as at Belle Cour, Wingfield but they were not usually fully glazed. They normally had shutters, louvres, or vertical slats. Timber lintels were often used in stone buildings to spread

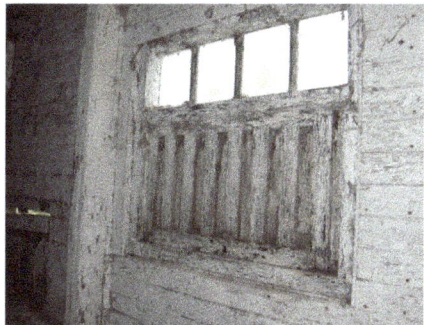

left: Shuttered window, 16th century stable at Westwood Manor, Westwood.
right: Hit and miss stable window, Lower Bridmore, Donhead St. Mary.

the load of the wall over the opening as was the case at Ganbrook Farm, Atworth. Windows with 'hit-and-miss' ventilation in the lower part were popular in the 19th century.

Lofts

A LOFT OR 'tallet' was a useful feature, giving ready access to fodder, utilising the roof space and sometimes housing the groom but it was by no means always provided. There was a view in the 19th century that open roofs were preferable, providing more air and ventilation for the horses. An alternative to a dormer window for the loft was to have a circular pitching hole.

The features inside the stable

C ARTHORSE STABLES WERE usually more open in their interior layout than nag stables.

left: Mays Farm, Hullavington. The farm had 250 acres of arable and nine working horses in 1916.
right: Chisbury Lane Farm, Little Bedwyn in about 1938.

left: Webbs Farm, Chiseldon. right: Lower Easton Farm, Corsham.

In riding horse stables there were usually stall divisions between the horses. They varied through time and according to the wealth of the owner. They were often ramped in an elegant curve. An early 18th century stable at Keevil has stall partitions of vertical planks with acorn finials on the heel-posts. An ornate example at Church Farm, Wingfield has a horse's head as a finial. 19th century stall divisions had narrower planks, often with iron bars at the top.

left: Stall divisions: Manor Farm, Erlestoke. right: Manor Farm, Stockton.

left: East Combe Farm, Castle Combe, a home farm of about 1840.
right: Mill Farm, West Lavington

left: Church Farm, Wingfield right: 19th century stable, Rodmead Farm, Maiden Bradley.

The mangers were usually wooden and set at the level of the horse's head. The horse was tied to a ring in the manger. There were also loose boxes where the animals were not tied but could move about freely. They were used mainly for foaling or for box-rest during recovery from injury or illness. These had corner mangers, often in the 19th century made of cast iron.

The hay racks in the Keevil stable mentioned above are of planks with horizontal applied strips giving a moulded or reeded effect. Usually there were staves which in section resemble the diamond mullions of an early window. Where there was a loft above, there were no floorboards above the racks so that hay could be pitch-forked down for the horses. This was known as a hay-drop. Sometimes there was a hay rack at the end of the manger.

left: Fully-boarded manger and hay rack above, Manger Barn, Lacock.
centre: Ganbrook Farm, Atworth. Note the bottom rail of the hayrack and the top in the beam, the original manger and the drain hole in the south wall.
right: Manger for one animal, St. Mary's House, Orcheston.

Corner mangers at Easton Court Farm and Lower Easton Farm, Corsham

There were often small recesses in the stable wall; keeping holes for grooming equipment or places to put a lamp. Where a long journey to market was involved, grooming might have to start at 4 o'clock in the morning. Some storage space was always provided for harness. This was usually in the form of wooden harness hooks. These were sometimes extremely 'rustic' being of timber naturally grown in a curved shape. As with other fittings, iron was increasingly used in the 19th century.

Nag stables of the 19th century often had a separate tack room partitioned off from the stalled part of the stable. It was usually lined with tongue and groove pine boarding throughout and often had a small fireplace so the harness could be dried off and the groom could clean it in winter in some comfort. If there was no outside stair, access to the loft was by a ladder usually set flat against an interior wall. This saved space and kept it out of the way of the horses.

left: Hooks with harness remaining at Stanley Abbey Farm, Bremhill.
right: Keeping hole below hooks at Mays Farm, Hullavington.

left: Harness room adjoining the stable, Ugford Farm, Burcombe Without.
centre: Loft ladder, Dudmore Lodge, Aldbourne. right: Hooks, Eastrop Farm, Highworth.

The beams across the stable ceiling were usually well finished with chamfers and simple stops. Their size and the width of the chamfers varied over time like the beams in houses.

The stable floor was designed on a slight slope for drainage and with a rough surface to prevent the iron shoes of the animals slipping. Pitched stones might be used or in the 19th century specially-made paving bricks with indentations on the surface. Several types are commonly found, usually of grey colour. They may have been nationally available rather than locally made. The cobbles or bricks used inside the stable extended outside the stable door forming an apron. Nearby there might also be a set of stone mounting blocks to assist riders. These included ladies in dresses,

Stone floor, Westleaze Farm, Wroughton.

people riding pillion, the elderly, the infirm, the short or those with large horses. Most of the blocks are double width for the rider's two feet but some are single width.

left: Pitch paving outside the former stable door, Pinkney Court Farm, Sherston.
right: Mounting block outside the traphouse, Chapel Farm, Blunsdon.

Housing for Cattle

Oxhouses

IN WILTSHIRE A few medieval buildings which housed cattle survive. Every farm had oxen or a share in the oxen which were vital for ploughing and other heavy work. They were often housed in a combination building with a stable at one end. There was a wide entrance for oxen in the front wall and the window openings were small. There were often lofts over either the cattle or horse sections. The lists of farm buildings at rectories in 1649 give an oxhouse at Sherston, a stable and oxhouse of 4 bays at Cricklade,. The list also includes oxhouses in 1695 and 1715 at Bradford-on-Avon and Winsley.

A very early surviving example is the Manger Barn, tree-ring dated 1359, at Manor Farm, Lacock, a monastic farm. It was originally timber-framed and comprised a small hay barn at the east end, an oxhouse in the middle and a stable in the west lean-to or 'cut' end.

A 3-bay cruck building at Manor Farm, Stockton is likely also to have been an oxhouse, then perhaps a carthorse stable. Stable fittings suggest that in the early 19th century it became a riding horse stable with an attached coach house. From the early 16th century another likely example is the long range attached to the barn at

Oxhouse, Manor Farm, Lacock. A timber-framed structure of 1359, the walls rebuilt in stone. A small hay barn at the left end has a re-used cruck truss of 1252-77. Nag stable at the right end and the central part when rebuilt in stone became a carthorse stable.

Westwood Manor, Westwood. An example with a stable is a 17th century oxhouse at Church Farm, Wingfield, the former manor house, and there is a remarkable timber-framed survival of similar date at Fyfield Manor, Milton Lilbourne.

Two other examples, perhaps of slightly later date are at Home Farm, Teffont Evias and Slades Farm, Box.

left: Probable 16th century oxhouse adjoining the barn at Westwood Manor, Westwood. An original internal doorway to the barn would have been used to bring in hay. The porch was added.
right: Stable in the gable end of the 17th century oxhouse, Church Farm, Wingfield.

left: Timber-framed oxhouse, Fyfield Manor, Milton Lilbourne.
right: Oxhouse, Home Farm, Teffont Evias, Teffont.

Front and rear views of the oxhouse, Slades Farm, Box. Small windows give a dark interior and the doorway is wide.

Accommodation for milking cows

F EW MILKING CATTLE were kept until the 18th century. A mid-16th century farmer at Whitley, Melksham Without had 4 oxen, 5 kine (cows), 4 bullocks of 2 years of age and 5 yearlings. In 1603 a husbandman at Semington had 3 oxen, 4 kine and 4 heifers. A wealthy farmer at Corsham in 1666 had 7 plough oxen and 12 cows and steers.

Milking cows were sometimes kept in a similar way to oxen. The Pembroke Survey of 1631 found many examples of cowhouses, mostly either separate buildings or combined with a stable or a barn. When a size is given, the separate buildings were usually between 1 and 4 bays long. Enclosed cowhouses were still being used in the 18th and 19th centuries though to a lesser extent.

When the term 'cow stall' was used in documents it applied to open-fronted buildings. The local name was a skilling or skillin and the word is still used. It is clear from old sources that it originally meant a lean-to building open on one side. The writer Richard Jefferies said that it was also used for the pent roof on posts outside farmhouse dairies, Thomas Davis used it for lean-tos behind cottages and in Berkshire it is used for open-fronted cart sheds.

There was a cow stall at Preshute rectory in 1649. Although shelter sheds of this kind were being built right through the 18th century there was a great increase in their numbers due to the farming improvements of the end of the century especially from about 1770 onwards. Davis said that South Wiltshire farms usually had a cow shed for the cattle that were wintered in the yard on straw and if possible there was a drinking pool there for them. In the dairy and grazing parts of North Wiltshire he said that the cowsheds, calf houses and milking yards were in general on a much superior plan to those in many other areas. He also said that landlords were encouraged to make

This cowshed at Cloatley Manor, Hankerton has a datestone of 1706. It is the earliest dated cow stall in Wiltshire.

such conveniences by the 'remarkable neat stile' in which they were almost uniformly kept throughout this district. By the end of the 19th century some farms in North Wiltshire had four or five sets of shelter sheds and miscellaneous other buildings for cattle. Sheds for over-wintering were also constructed away from the farmyard in the fields. Sometimes they were part of a field barn complex and sometimes not.

Cloately Manor, Hankerton has the first known dated example in the county of an open-fronted shelter shed for cattle and it still has a stable at one end. The datestone of 1706 shows the pride of the new owner in constructing such a fine modern farmstead.

The stone-pillared front, perhaps an innovation at that date, continued in the limestone area of the county until the mid-19th century. The pillars could be of ashlar or rubble stone, square or circular, and straight or tapering. Occasionally they were moulded at the top. Later in the 19th century there were circular brick pillars using bull-nosed bricks and a few estates built ranges with arched openings.

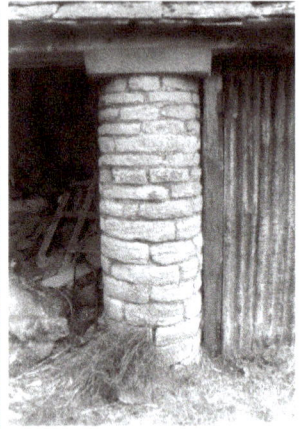

left: 18th century cowshed at Mays Farm, Hullavington. A probable calf shed at the end.
right: An 18th century cowshed at Starveall Farm, Chippenham Without.

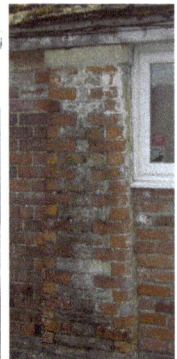

left: Cowshed of c.1840 at East Combe Farm, Castle Combe, an estate farm for Castle Combe Manor.
right: 19th century brick pier with bull-nosed bricks, former cowshed at Fowlswick Farm, Chippenham Without.,

Square stone pillars at Belle Cour Farm, Wingfield.

Over most of the county it was more usual to have wooden posts on padstones along the open front. The padstones were similar to the bases of staddle stones and prevented the posts from rotting. In the late 19th century hollow cast-iron posts were sometimes used.

18th and some 19th century sheds had curved bracing along the front of the shed. In the 19th century others had 'pillow braces' above the posts. The tiebeams of the roof trusses were often braced underneath at the front of the shed. At the end of the 19th century the braces were sometimes shaped.

There was sometimes vertical boarding between the posts, some being hinged gates and some fixed. This stopped short of the ground to keep clear of manure and there was also a gap above to give plenty of ventilation. Edward Peters mentions that this type of cowhouse was common in Worcestershire and it is also found elsewhere.

Field cowshed, Seend, formerly thatched and convex braces to the tiebeams.

Iron posts, Salisbury Plain farm.

Pillow brace, Lower Easton Farm, Corsham and brace to the tiebeam.

Inside the shelter shed there was normally a wooden manger at floor level and posts to which the animals were tied using iron rings on chains. This enabled them to stand up or lie down. Peter Nicholson wrote that the posts were locally called 'ram

above left: Postcard from a dairy farm. Mangers at Manor Farm, Erlestoke (below left) and Upper Baynton Farm, Edington (above right).
below right: Mays Farm, Hullavington. The cowshed was re-roofed with a king bolt truss in the late 19th century and the interior adapted to follow 1930s government instructions for tubular stall divisions and concrete mangers.

poles'. Between groups of stalls there were sometimes partitions. Several bratticed examples have been recorded. There is sometimes ventilation in the rear wall above the mangers. Behind the cattle in the floor there was usually a drainage channel or the whole floor was at a lower level behind the standings.

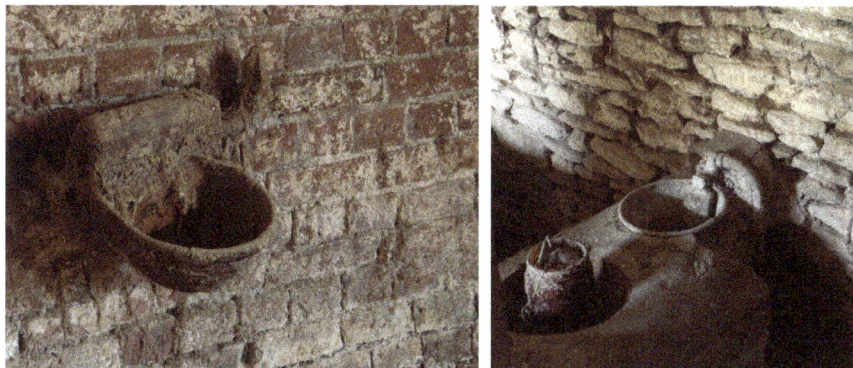

Water bowls: Lower Easton Farm, Corsham (left) and Manor Farm, Erlestoke (right).

left: Bratticing at Manor Farm, Hilperton.
right: Sliding door between stalls at Eastrop Farm, Highworth.

The roof structures of shelter sheds were usually tiebeam trusses with V struts or kingpost trusses (see Upper Baynton above). In the late 19th century there might be king bolt trusses or king rod trusses.

Rear wall ventilation. Rodmead Farm, Maiden Bradley.

Several enclosed loose boxes were sometimes attached to the end of the shelter shed for young stock or for fattening. There were also calf sheds, either separate small buildings or attached to the side of the barn. On larger farms there were bull pens. At all periods use was also made of space within the barn.

left: Bull pen, Salisbury Plain farm, with opening to fill the trough without entering. right: Cattle ties and partition, barn at Lower Bridmore Farm, Donhead St. Mary.

Calf shed, Widbrook Farm, Bradford-on-Avon, probably 1834-5.

Accommodation for Pigs and Poultry

Before the 16th century pigs were usually given access to woodland where they fed on acorns and rooted for themselves. Later on sties and yards were increasingly used and the pigs were fed on the whey left after cheese-making. There is not a great deal of evidence about Wiltshire pig keeping in the 16th century but it is likely that with the great growth in dairying and the loss of woodland it became practical to keep pigs close to the farmhouse. A sty is shown outside the dairy in a 1695 plan of Avebury Manor. Bacon came to be an important product of the county. There were bacon curing chambers next to farmhouse fireplaces and salting equipment is included in inventories.

From the early 17th century some sties are mentioned in documents and they are often in association with henhouses, a combination found in other counties and abroad. The theory was that pigs kept the foxes away. The Trowbridge Rectory terrier of 1671 lists a 'dovehouse and pigsty adjoining' and 'another pigsty and an henhouse'. At Frankley, Bradford-on-Avon in 1695 there was a pig barton and the next building mentioned is a henhouse. These references suggest the first pigsty might have been under the dovecote and that the other was a combined building. The pig barton was a small yard for loose pigs but it might also have contained sties. As a late example a piggery 'with a henhouse above' was specified for a farmstead on Salisbury Plain in 1863.

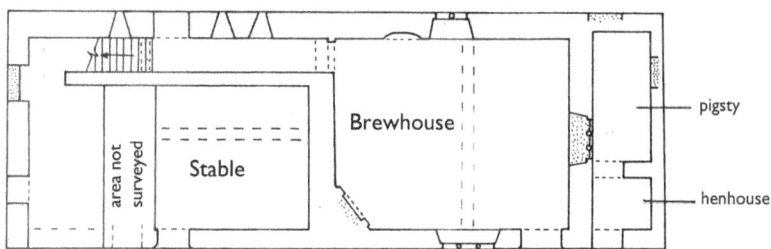

PARISH ROOMS

CORSHAM

WILTSHIRE

The Warden's pigsty of 1668 at the Hungerford Almshouses, Corsham. A poultry house was attached at an early date. (©Crown Copyright. Historic England Archive)

The earliest dated pigsty still existing in the county is probably that at the Hungerford Almshouses, Corsham, constructed between 1668 and 1672. It was for the use of the schoolmaster/warden and is shown on the original plan of the complex. It is a lean-to structure against the end of the brewhouse/stable range with a round-arched doorway. There is no surviving enclosure but a low doorway through the outer wall of the almshouse complex gave access to the common outside. A henhouse was added soon after and the hens may also have been let out on to the common.

Hungerford Almshouses, Corsham: Pigsty (above left); Poultry house (above right); Exit hole viewed from the common (below left).   17th century pigsty with a hen loft above at Cromhall Farm, Kington St. Michael (below right).

Another early survival is the henhouse over a pigsty at Cromhall Farm, Kington St. Michael. The square doorway may be an alteration from an arched entrance.

In South Wales and Somerset, some early stone pigsties were circular with a corbelled roof. Circular dovecotes gave way to rectangular dovecotes in Wiltshire and it is possible that the small rectangular houses for pigs which are sometimes found in the county had circular antecedents.

With the growth of dairying and with more pigs being kept, the most common layout was in a row with each sty having its enclosure. The enclosures in the limestone area were sometimes made with large slabs of stone known as orthostatic walls. At Ashton Keynes where the slabs are also used for garden walls, they were called 'pig

'Small house' pigsties: Street Farm, Compton Bassett and Chapel Farm, Blunsdon.

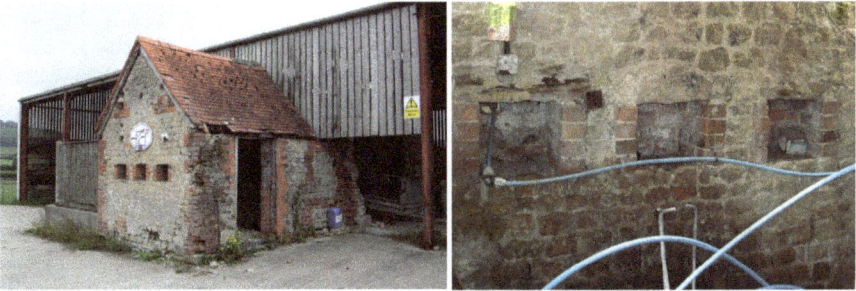

One unit remaining of a pigsty with nest boxes for poultry at Rodmead Farm, Maiden Bradley. The outer enclosure has also gone.

Entry hole and poultry loft in a pigsty at Derriads Farm, Chippenham.

walls'. At a few model farms like Milbourne Farm, Corsham, the sties were more architectural with detailing matching other buildings. Brick pigsties seem to have been a 19th century development. The doorways of these are usually arched.

Pigsties of stone with brick dressings and brick dividing walls. Home Farm, Biddestone.

Stone pigsties with arched doorways and capped walls, Colerne Down Farm, Colerne.

Stone slab walls; Lanes End Farm, Gastard, Corsham (left)
and a 19th century range at Pond Close Farm, The Ridge, Corsham (right).

Former pigsty with rubble stone walls and ashlar dressings. It formerly had brick interior dividing walls, continued outside and capped with blue semi-circular bricks. The outer pen wall was of stone with semi-circular capping stones. The adjoining meal house (and stable facing the other way) is of similar design with Diocletian (semicircular) windows. Milbourne Farm, Corsham.

Sometimes the pigsty was one of the lean-to buildings against the side of the barn. There was also a later plan type where the pig pens were inside the building with a feeding passage and there was no outside run. This was the case in later provision at May's Farm, Hullavington and at a farm on Salisbury Plain. The 1898 sale particulars for Manor House, Steeple Langford include 'Two piggeries with feeding passage'.

Brick pigsties, Catridge Farm, Lacock.

A former pigsty against the barn with poultry entrances at Mays Farm, Hullavington, the doorway has been enlarged.

Late 19th century new sties (above) with a feeding passage (below left), Mays Farm, Hullavington. Pig pens and feeding passage at a Salisbury Plain farm (below right).

Another variation, found along the south of the county, has the pigsties built into the ground floor of a two-storey building with other functions. At Ham Cross Farm, Tisbury, a model farm for the Wyndhams of Phillips House, Dinton, the granary has a pigsty below with elliptical arches. At Westwood Farm, Semley, Sedgehill and Semley parish, the pigsties are in the end wall of a range which includes a stable and cartshed and there is a hen house above.

Inside the sty, ventilation was sometimes by a shuttered window or a ventilation slit in the end wall. Often the doorway was the only source of ventilation. Whey was sometimes delivered direct from the dairy via a chute or there was a chute through the front wall of the enclosure to a trough.

In a row of sties a partition wall often rose to eaves level between the separate houses. At the end of the range there might be a meal house with a copper for boiling up potatoes and other food (see Milbourne Farm above). Various methods were used to provide a creep area to prevent sows from lying on the piglets. At Cloatley Manor, Hankerton there were the remains of an elaborate arrangement of rustic poles and a slab of stone inside the sty. At Mays Farm, Hullavington and Pound Farm, Bromham there was a more orderly wooden structure.

Westwood Farm, Semley, Sedgehill and Semley (above). Pigsties are incorporated at the right end of the range. Poultry entrances in the front wall (below left). Doorway for the pigs in the end wall (below right)

left: Wooden shuttered window, Street Farm, Compton Bassett.
right: Iron feeding chute in the front wall, Barton Farm, Bradford-on-Avon.

Today traditional sties are rarely used for their original purpose and they are not as easily converted as larger buildings. Their fate is often demolition or use as a garden store.

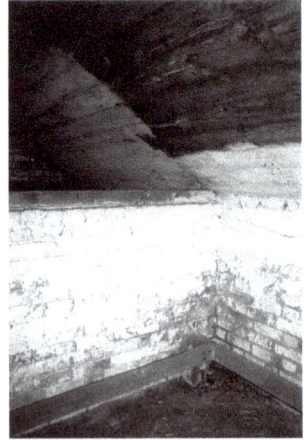

Frameworks to protect the piglets: Mays Farm, Hullavington and Pound Farm, Bromham.

Separate provision for poultry

THE PROVISION FOR poultry was sometimes separate from the pigsties or dovecote. At Pinkney Court, Sherston, a long narrow building is attached to the end of a barn with a granary beyond. It has nesting holes for geese at floor level and smaller holes for hens above. At Elm House Farm, Biddestone a white-washed room formed between the house and a

Nesting boxes on both sides of the room called 'Hen roost' in sale particulars of 1918, Elm House Farm, Biddestone.

Nest boxes for hens at waist level and below, at floor level, one of the larger recesses for geese or ducks, Pinkney Court, Sherston.

Goose nesting boxes at the side of the front lawn, Ridge Farm, Neston.

'skilling' has 12 roosts on one side wall and eight on the other. It was described as 'Hen Roost' in sale particulars of 1919. In all these examples the wooden ladder, probably a narrow plank of wood with attached strips, has gone.

From the late 19th century portable (wheeled) timber poultry houses were used. Some were manufactured locally by firms such as Barretts at Wroughton and Iles, followed by W.H. Hill & Son, at Stratton St. Margaret.

Dovecotes

T HESE ARE FULLY described in John McCann's *The Dovecotes and Pigeon Lofts of Wiltshire.* A recent find not included in the book is at Pickwick Manor, Corsham.

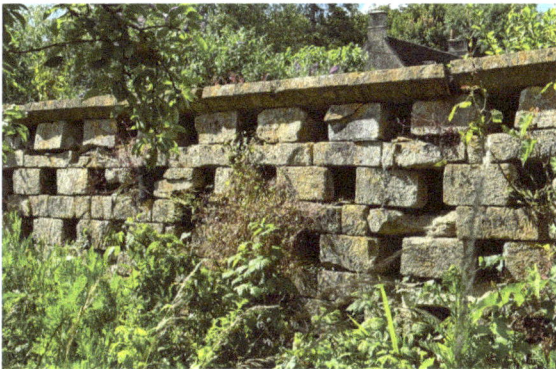

Interior of the dovecote at Pickwick Manor, Corsham.

The building was square and the one remaining section of wall is unusual in being of dry-stone construction.

Endnotes

1   WAM 81 (1987), pp.80-90

Sheephouses

S HEEPHOUSES WERE ONCE widespread in Wiltshire where there were huge flocks of sheep on the downs and also large numbers in the vales and Cotswold region. It 1813 there were still estimated to be 500,000 sheep in the county. The sheephouse was a building made of local materials, with perhaps internal pens, in which sheep could lamb, shearing could take place and the sheep were protected and fed hay during severe weather.

Documentary evidence starts in the medieval period when some at least were cruck-built. St Swithin's Priory, Winchester placed three forks (crucks) is a sheephouse at Overton Priors in either 1271/2 or 1291/2 and renewed a larger one with eight couples of forks in the same manor in 1317/18. Badbury at Chiseldon, a manor of Glastonbury Abbey, had in 1189 the capacity to keep 250 sheep. By the early 14th century it had 320 sheep and accounts of 1302-35 refer to a sheephouse. In 1334-5 extensive work was done to its roof. Shaftesbury Abbey built a new sheephouse in their Tisbury manor in 1392 and 150 feet of ridge tiles (stone crests) were brought from their quarry at Bradford-on-Avon. This may have been the sheephouse at East Knoyle mentioned in the Pembroke estate survey of 1570. The site is now called Sheephouse Farm. At their Bradford manor in 1367, 15 acres of wheat were sown in 'Sheephouscroft'. In the 14th or early 15th century the Tropenell Cartulary recorded that 'there is a shepehous, grounde and land in the feld of Maydenbradeley, called Balles shepehouse, now adowne.'

There are many post-medieval place-name and documentary references showing that sheephouses remained common, often situated in meadows. The Pembroke estate survey of 1631-2 has: Sheephouse Bottom, Broad Chalke; Sheephouse Mead, Dinton; part of a close of meadow 'wherein is a sheep house' in a copyhold farm at Stanton St. Bernard; four closes of meadow with a sheep house in one at another copyhold farm at the same village; a barn of 3 rooms (bays), with an oxhouse and a sheephouse at one end at East Mead, Bishopstone South. In the 18th century at Little Chalfield, Atworth, a field called Eight Acres was described as 'by the sheephouse'. In 1764 William Parsons was found dead in a sheephouse at Melksham.

In the late 20th century farmers were advised that a building 60 feet long by 23 feet wide and 8-11 feet to the eaves would house 93 sheep. This seems quite comparable to the medieval provision. A sheephouse at Norton St. Philip, just over the border in Somerset, in 1652, measured 120 feet long and 23 feet broad. Historically, the eaves were much lower than today making the building more wind-proof. In Cumbria barns and stables with provision for sheep have a low door, 1.22m (4 feet) tall or even less. Some sheep houses still existing in Gloucestershire in 1983 had solid

Shepherds of Barton Farm, Marlborough with hurdled sheep. In the background, a long sheephouse with an open front on poles and a roof of thatch or solid thatch. (Gray & James Marlborough in Old Photographs)

thatch roofs where furze or brushwood was piled over flat ceilings of hurdles and then thatched. Something similar is shown in the background of an old photograph from the Marlborough area.

The historian Camden (writing in the late 16th/early 17th century) described sheep cots in Gloucestershire and neighbouring counties as being long ranges of buildings, three or four storeys high with low ceilings and a slope at one end of each floor, reaching to the next 'by which the sheep were enabled to reach the topmost one'. This unusual arrangement sounds similar to a livestock lorry but there is no evidence of anything like this in Wiltshire.

Some sheephouses remained in Wiltshire in the 19th century and just a few in remote places have lasted to the present day. Wiltshire Buildings Record has found three; a dilapidated building at East Knoyle, another at West Kennett, Avebury and

East Knoyle sheephouse with walls of vertical planks, a hipped roof (formerly thatched) and interior timber partitions.

one in the south of the county. The East Knoyle building was in a collapsed state in 1993. It was a long, low building with eaves 1.52 m (5 feet) high. The walls had vertical staggered boarding, probably of elm, the 4-bay roof had been thatched and was hipped at both ends. The interior had one end partitioned off, also with vertical boarding. The overall size was about 10.6m (nearly 35 feet) long and nearly 5m (16 feet) wide. It was situated about half a mile from the farmhouse in the corner of a field near the end of a lane and carpentry details suggested a c.1800 date. This may be similar in construction to the sheephouse at Bratton described as 'new boarded' by three men in 1741.

The West Kennett building was recorded in 1990. It was again in an isolated position, on the side of a valley in downland. Its roof was also hipped at both ends. It had been weather-boarded and thatched. The roof carpentry suggested a late 18th century date.

The third example, found very recently in South Wilts is situated by a lane, near the farm but separate from the main yard. It is 50m (98' 6') long, 1.75m (5' 9") to the eaves and about 4m (just over 13') deep. It too is hipped at both ends. It is constructed of cob with some brick repairs and has the remains of thatch. The original roof is now covered with galvanised iron sheets. The section at one end has a boarded floor and the farmer suggested this area was for use during shearing.

A South Wiltshire sheephouse of the late 18th or early 19th century. Front facing the field and rear by a track.

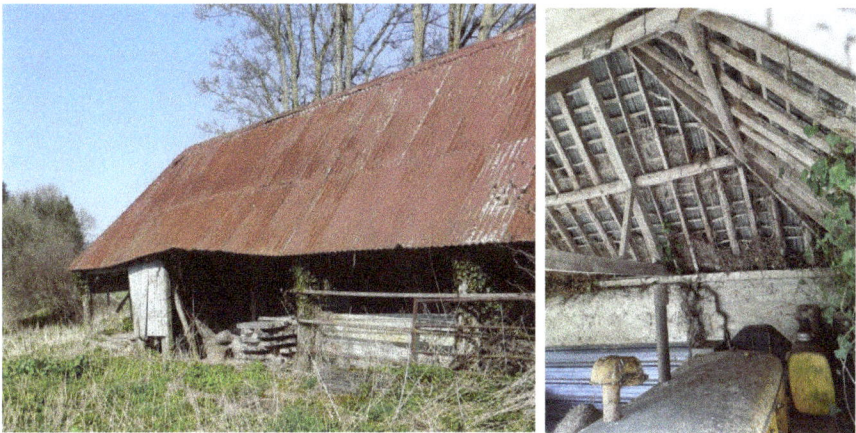

The west end with plank floor and the interior of the east end with some thatch remaining.

Sheep washes

S HEEP WASHING TO clean the wool before shearing was carried out in a river, stream or pond. The practice was wide-spread in Wiltshire and the surrounding counties of Gloucestershire, Bath and North-east Somerset and Dorset. For convenience, a stone basin was often constructed, about 3m in diameter and 1.5 m deep. The flow and depth of water through was controlled by sluices at each end and there was a sloping escape ramp. The sheep were pushed under the water with poles or crooks. Sheepwash Lane at Wylye led to a wash on the river Wylye. An enclosure would be made both sides of the river. The river would be partly dammed leaving a small area in the middle for water to escape. At Cloatley Manor, Hankerton, a series of walls adjoining a pond (made out of part of the moat) may have been used as a sheep wash. Others are at Woolley, Bradford-on-Avon and West Kington, Nettleton. Most built examples date from the late 18th or 19th century.

Sheep dipping is a different process. It began in about 1830 and was carried out to remove insect pests by immersing the sheep in a solution of disinfectant in a wooden trough. Evidence of fencing to funnel the sheep to the dipping place still exists on some farms, for example in the yard at West Kennett Farm, Avebury.

Three men sheep dipping in a trough at Lower Easton Farm, Corsham, c. 1920.

Goat houses

A CCORDING TO AN inventory there was a goat house at Bewley Court, Lacock in 1418 with 40 goats. (WAM 81, p.67)

Dairies and Cheeserooms

B ARTON FARM AT Bradford-on-Avon had a dairy in 1367. It was in a range at one side of the farmyard with the brewhouse and malthouse. The inventory shows it had a 'dome' for making and pressing cheese, rotating shelves of four round stepped boards to store cheeses, a long shelf for cheeses and two stools. Similar equipment was still being used centuries later.

The majority of dairies in Wiltshire were either in a back room of the farmhouse or in an attached wing, next to the farmhouse with a brewhouse beyond. A smaller number were separate buildings. These often resemble small houses. They can be either one, one and a half or two storeys high and were larger in the cheese-producing areas where the upper floor was the cheese room. They have always been seen as suitable

Dairy window with zinc mesh and horizontal shutter, Malt House, Wilsford (above left). Manor Farm, Erlestoke; dairy attached to the farmhouse (above right), dairy window and barred cheeseroom window (below).

for conversion to accommodation for farm workers and they may even have an original chimney stack for the fireplace or stove which kept the cheeseroom at a steady temperature in winter.

It was important, on the other hand, to keep the dairy cool. Windows are small and often shaded by a veranda. They were often made of mesh to keep out insects. Cheeses were valuable produce and were protected by locked doors and bars on the windows.

Inside the dairy there was a long working top, shelving and equipment.

Slate Farm, Wanborough; brick worktop and shelf above, general view with Carson cheese press.

Large estates often built ornamental detached dairies, usually still incorporating some kind of covered area where the milk could be brought and utensils put to dry and air. The most architectural example is probably the one at New Wardour Castle, Tisbury of 1774. Another at Conock Manor, Chirton, of 1817, has a 'rustic' design.

In the 18th century when pressure for cheese storage increased with the

Slate shelf with iron support, probably pre-1866, Wylye Valley farm.

left: Dairy of 1774, New Wardour Castle, Tisbury. right: Picturesque dairy of 1817 at Conock Manor Chirton, by Nottinghamshire architect Richard Ingleman. The veranda is of rustic wood with knots of rough bark nailed on.

Conock Manor, Chirton, brick working top and glazed tiles inside.

growth of the industry, other, sometimes high quality, rooms were taken over within the house and the attic might be given shelving.

Hoists were used to lift the heavy hard cheeses to the cheese storage areas. They are increasingly rare survivals and each one recorded has been different in design.

In the cheeseroom, storage was on long broad shelving known as rack and tack. The carpentry of this varies. The earliest seen was probably that at Oxenleaze Farm, Holt. It was still provided in 1881 at the new Stanley Abbey Farm, Bremhill.

Brick dairy with veranda, Pyatts Farm, Keevil and cheese racks in the farmhouse attic.

Dairy, attached to northwest corner of Heywood Farm, Kington St Michael (above left). Interior with zinc meshed meat safe on the wall (above). Remnants of cheese storage racks in the farmhouse attic (left).

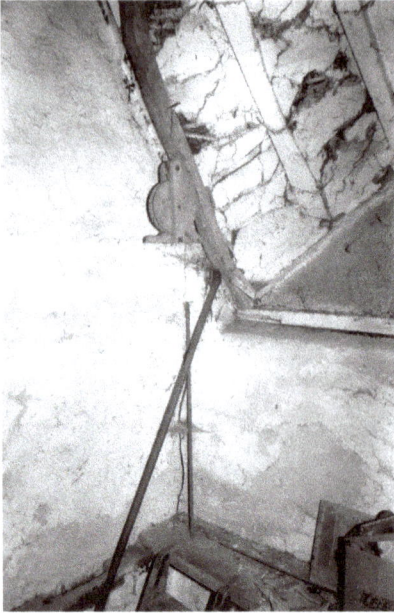

Hoists; Slate Farm, Wanborough (above left) and Manor Farm, Erlestoke (above right). 'Rack and tack' shelving for cheeses; Oxenleaze Farm, Holt (left) and Slades Farm, Box (below), where It was on both sides of the cheeseroom with probably a double-sided rack in the middle of the room.

Dairy equipment

THE RANGE OF dairy equipment is illustrated by the description in the farm sale of Rowcroft Farm, Seend in 1841. The farmhouse was demolished in 1938. Some of the terms used are the same as in 17th century inventories; cowel or coule (tub), kiver (barrel), tack (shelf).

'Excellent double-box cheese press with leads; also a single-box ditto; capital brass cheese cowel, stand, tongs and sieve; small wood cheese tub; new 37 gallon barrel, butter churn and stand; upright ditto; 2 good double whey leads and stands; oval butter kiver; brass milk pan, tin milk warmer; 30 large and small cheese vats and followers; salting bench; 3 milk pails; very excellent scale beam and scales; small beam and scales; number of brass and iron weights; also a lot of brown milk ware, milk barrel, cheese tacks etc.'

A book of 1886, *The Equipment of the Farm* by Burness, Morton and Murray, explains the dairy implements found at that time to process milk, cream and butter and which were still used in the 20th century. These included milk strainers – wooden or tin-plate bowls with hair cloth or wire-cloth bottoms; milk coolers with two corrugated plates up between which cold water flowed with the milk flowing down both sides into a pail below. There were also lactometers indicating the percentage

Bowden Hill Farm, Lacock; the two-storey dairy (top left), interior with covered vat (top right), slate shelf (bottom left, and cheese press (bottom right).

thickness of the cream – four glass tubes in a frame; vessels for throwing up cream – 20 inches in diameter and 6 inches deep; stone shelves or tables for setting the pans in cold or hot water; skimming dishes to remove the cream. There were also churns or barrels to make butter and churns to convey milk to outside processing or sale. They said the dairy should have a shelf or bench, about 20 inches wide, carried round the room on which to set the milk pans.

For cheese-making, a vat was required for curdling the milk with rennet. After the curd was broken up and the whey removed or in the case of Cheddar cheese the curd was heated in a double-sided steam vat, it was then put in a mould and pressed.

A fully equipped two-storey dairy and cheeseroom of 19th century date was recorded at Bowden Hill, Lacock in 1989. The contents had been abandoned when cheese-making ceased in the 1930s.

Bowden Hill Farm; wooden cheese mould (top left), butter churn and followers (top right), curd cutters (bottom left) and stove and racks in the cheeseroom above (bottom right).

Brewhouses, bakehouses and wash-houses

Wiltshire brewhouses were most often in a wing attached to the farmhouse, beyond the dairy. Mays Farm, Hullavington is one of many examples of this. They could also be free standing. In inventories they might be called the 'back kitchen', 'out-kitchen' or occasionally the 'kiln house'.

left: Single storey brewhouse between the dairy (to right) and woodhouse (to left), May's Farm, Huillavington. right: Brewhouse, late 17th or early 18th century, at East Barton, Keevil.

A 16th century brewhouse with its fittings can be visited at Lacock Abbey, Lacock where it is on the far side of the stable yard well away from the house. A rebuilding agreement for Norton Bavant Manor House in December 1641 specified that the brewhouse should be of sound timber, the walls filled with brick, of five bays, with ovens, kiln and furnace. Usually the building was multi-purpose. A 1689 document from Atworth mentions the 'use of my brewhouse to wash and to brew'. Baking was another activity which took place there and the farm workers could use the building for their mid-day meal and for the celebration of 'harvest homes'. The rooms therefore had a similar function to the servants' halls of the great houses. In a few instances when they were not open to the rafters, there was a sleeping room for farm workers above. This was the case at Dudmore Lodge, Aldbourne.

Fittings

The fittings of a brewhouse usually included a large open fireplace with an oven, a brewing 'furnace' on one side and a washing copper on the other. They usually have an end stack though a few have a lateral stack. The oven usually protrudes

Fireplace in the 'Men's House' at Dudmore Lodge, Aldbourne (left) and staircase to the sleeping accommodation above (centre). Note the hat pegs and supports for a roller towel. External stone-tiled oven to the brewhouse with lateral stack at Cogswells, Tytherton Lucas, Bremhill (right).

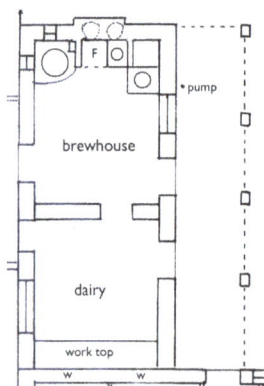

Plan of the brewhouse at Slate Farm, Wanborough (left). There is a brewing vat to the left of the fireplace, two ovens in the fireplace and a washing copper to the right. Outside in the dairy pentice is the well pump (page 23). Brewhouse, Slate Farm, Wanborough, looking towards the brewing vat (right). There is a clothes-drying rack in the ceiling.

Fireplace in the brewhouse at Mays Farm, Hullavington and the oven, protruding behind into the wood store.

beyond the building. Inside, or just outside, there was usually a well pump with a D-shaped stone trough.

Use as a dower house

WILLS OF THE 17th century sometimes instruct that the widow was to be given sleeping accommodation in the upper room of a brewhouse and she had the right to use the fire downstairs for cooking and warmth. At Holt Manor, the late 16th or 17th century brewhouse was probably used in this way as a dower house. The facade has architectural features and the right-hand part of the building has a separate ground floor fireplace. There is a good quality fireplace in the room above the main fireplace. For the brewhouse, there was once a separate entrance door in the west wall, keeping the two functions of the building partly separate.

Old Beer House, Holt Manor, Holt. The doorway, the brewing fireplace (partly filled in) and the first floor fireplace above.

Bakehouses

IN A FEW instances the bakehouse was a separate building from the brewhouse. At Leigh House Farm, Bradford-on-Avon the oven was larger than usual and it was used commercially by the end of the 17th century. The small single storey building at Bolehyde Manor, Chippenham Without was in addition to a brewhouse of similar date.

Early bakehouse, Leigh House Farm, Bradford-on-Avon (top left). Note the small monolithic fireplace window. The building was detached originally but was later joined to the farmhouse. Inside (top right), the fireplace was between an oven to the left (with moulded lintel) and perhaps a boiler to the right. An external bread oven with large capping stone, of about 1700, Bolehyde Manor, Chippenham Without (left).

Wash-houses

AFTER BREWING CEASED, the building was often still used as a wash-house or for farm workers. Alternatively, the wash-house could be a small lean-to area.

Wash-house at Lower Bridmore Farm, Donhead St. Mary (left). It was formerly thatched. Wash-house at Mitchells Farm, Seend (centre). Stair to the granary and washing copper at the end of the dairy pentice, Slades Farm, Box (right).

Waggon sheds

A WAGGON OR wain was a large four-wheeled vehicle used to carry loads to market or bring in the crops at harvest-time. Its structure was complicated and varied with the area. It often carried the name of the farmer and the farm.

Between 1500 and 1750 farm transport became more important as subsistence farming was replaced by a more commercialised rural economy and more products were taken to the market for sale. Something larger than a cart was needed.

As a building type, the waggon shed can be traced back at least to 1649 when St Sampson's parsonage farm at Cricklade had 'a wainhouse' and the rectory at Sherston had a thatched 'wainhouse'. Their waggons were perhaps primarily for collecting tithes.

Waggon shed, Easton Court Farm, Corsham (left). It was formerly open between the pillars and thatched. This building at Barton Farm, Bradford-on-Avon (right) was open at both ends.

Waggon shed of cob at Manor Farm, Stockton. The queen post roof may be a 19th century repair.

Early waggon sheds were probably often simple buildings with open sides. More protection was provided when the sides were filled in and both ends left open. This had the advantage that the draught animals could be hitched at the far end the next time the waggon was needed. At a further stage of development just one end was open and the vehicle had to be reversed in.

The building was usually sited at the edge of the farmyard, adjacent to the fields or a track. The only fitting might be a keeping hole for grease. If the front was gabled, this was often boarded above eaves level. Thatched roofs were usually half-hipped and in the early 19th century there was a fashion for hipping.

Waggon sheds; Rodmead Farm, Maiden Bradley (left) and with hipped roof at Poplar Farm, Atworth (right).

Cart and implement sheds

A CART WAS a small two-wheeled vehicle. Tip-up carts which were used to carry and spread manure were in Wiltshire called 'dung potts'. Carts were essential for many jobs round the farm, originally even for bringing in hay and cereals. Cart sheds feature in the earliest lists of farm buildings. However, below manorial level most carriage may have originally been by pack animals. At his death in 1440, the bailiff of Castle Combe had an ironbound cart. By 1631 a number of copyholders on the Pembroke estates had 'cart houses'. At Netherhampton one had 'a cow house and a cart house with tallets overhead' and another 'a hovel to set a cart in'.

Cart shed with vertical boarded walls and a hipped solid thatch roof of furze lashed to poles. New Farm, Netheravon recorded in October, 1964.

Farm implements also had to be stored and these included tools, ladders, ploughs, rakes and harrows. Inventories show that smaller items were often kept in the house. In the 19th century many more types of machinery became available and Wiltshire had a thriving agricultural machinery industry. Very long cart sheds were constructed on large farms.

Some sheds were very cheaply constructed out of rough wood and thatch and examples are shown in old photographs and prints. However, the cart shed at New Farm, Netheravon recorded by Peter Nicholson in 1964, built of vertical boards with a solid thatch roof, offers a very neat appearance. It was a rare survival. Cob was quite often used, combined with a thatched roof.

Thatched cart shed, Alton Priors, Alton. The rear wall is still of cob. The wooden platform may have been used to roll a sheep over on its back to trim the feet.

From the 18th century, there were also some built of more expensive materials. Cylindrical stone pillars were used in the north of the county like those fronting cattle sheds. The range at Lower Hardenhuish Farm, Langley Burrell Without was part of a model farm and had a fine stone pillared front and a stone-tiled roof. At the home farm of Whaddon House, Hilperton there was a long range built of brick with stone dressings, rendered over and with a granary above. More commonly, however, throughout the county, the front had wooden posts, sometimes braced, and set on padstones.

Apart from the farm vehicles, in the 19th century the farmer often owned a trap or other light vehicle for his own transport. These were usually kept in an enclosed building. They were the forerunners of the modern garage and that often became their later use. Rather than build a separate building the solution was sometimes to insert partitions and put a door on an existing cart shed.

Late 18th century cart shed, Whaddon Grove Farm, Hilperton.

Timber-framed cart shed with slate roof and braced posts, Milbourne Farm, Corsham.

Cart shed and stable, Priory Farm, Burcombe Without. It was formerly thatched.

Cart shed, Manor Farm, Chitterne with some cob remaining at the rear. A shepherd's hut is parked to the right

Cart sheds; Rodmead Farm, Maiden Bradley (left) with internal partitions and with added doors, Great Lypiatt Farm, Corsham (right).

Trap houses; Chapel Farm, Blunsdon (left) and Elm Farm, Foxham, Bremhill (right).

Engine houses

AFTER HORSE MILLS the next stage of mechanisation was the introduction of the steam engine providing power for threshing or for preparing livestock feed by chaffing, pulping or slicing. The first portable engine was exhibited at Liverpool in 1841. They were in widespread use on large farms by the end of the 1850s. In Wiltshire this was mainly on arable farms in the south of the county. Being valuable, they were usually kept and operated in a lockable engine house. Portable engines could also be drawn by a horse between the engine shed and the rickyard to operate threshing machines. A portable steam engine is said to have been used in the cartway at Manor Farm, Chirton.

Engine houses are recognisable by their high doorways. Unlike waggon sheds they were positioned in the heart of the farmyard. This was usually next to the barn or feed preparation area with a line shaft through to drive machinery. They also have a smoke hood in the roof under which the engine's chimney is positioned.

Over time, portable engines were replaced, for indoor operations, by oil/petrol engines and then in the twentieth century by electric motors – and for threshing, by steam traction engines and later by tractors. These were often owned by contractors, who used them to tow large threshing machines from farm to farm. This continued until threshing machines were replaced by combine harvesters, first introduced into the UK during the 1920s. Farmsteads built after the adoption of the threshing machine no longer needed a great barn with a threshing floor.

The remains of gearing in the roof of the barn at Lower Easton Farm, Corsham.

The next development was steam ploughing using two engines, one each end of the field, and a plough. This was not widely adopted at first in Wiltshire where, in 1863, according to G. Fussell only six sets of equipment were in use, reducing to five in 1867. Because of the cost of the equipment and the expertise needed, this was chiefly done by contractors so no housing was required for the machinery on the farm. Between 1860 and 1920 in all 90 Fowler sets were purchased in the county with possibly some Howard roundabout steam ploughing sets and P.J. Parmiter direct ploughing engines. Horse ploughing continued alongside steam ploughing, until tractors came into widespread use in the interwar years and during the second world war, greatly reducing the need for farmstead stabling.

Engine sheds; with an engine at Manor Farm, Burcombe Without (top left) and at a Salisbury Plain farm (top right). Engine house adjoining the barn, Ugford Farm, Burcombe Without (bottom left). Drive shaft through to the barn at a Salisbury Plain farm (bottom right).

Wylye Valley farm; engine house at the end of the barn range with a roof vent and cart shed adjoining also with vents. A hoist above the cart shed to lift sacks to the granary.

Farm privies

To protect the privacy of the farmer's household, on larger farms there was an additional privy in the yard. It might be sited near the pigsties and it could drain into a cistern collecting waste from the pigsties, cowsheds or stables. Otherwise it might adjoin a drainage ditch. Where there are two holes this was for the exchange of buckets below for emptying. Sometimes there is a small additional hole for children to use.

Early 18th century privy, Lower Easton Farm, Corsham (left). Privies; Rodmead Farm, Maiden Bradley (centre) and Forest Farm, Melksham (right).

Privy seats; May's Farm, Hullavington (left) and with child's seat at Easton Court Farm, Corsham (right).

Smithies and workshops

O N THE LARGE farms in the south of the county there was sometimes a farm smithy to shoe horses and repair iron implements. These varied in size but are recognizable from their chimney and perhaps from the remains of the forge inside. Several late 19th century examples of iron windows have been recorded, probably in case of fire.

Smithy, Rodmead Farm, Maiden Bradley with a privy attached at the far end, and the forge inside.

Smithy and forge, Salisbury Plain farm.

Smithy and wheelwright's shop, Wylye Valley farm (above), and the forge (below left).

Twelve pane metal window with circular rose motifs on the crossings, carpenter's shop, Salisbury Plain farm (centre) and metal window at a Wylye valley farm (right).

Similarly on large farms there might be a carpenter's or wheelwright's shop with a work bench. Otherwise the bench was located in part of the barn or elsewhere. Every farm would have had a grindstone to sharpen tools but they rarely survive.

Work benches; at a Salisbury Plain farm (left), in the barn at Manor Farm, Chitterne (right) and in the tack room at Manor Farm, Erlestoke (opposite page, top).

Fuel stores

WOOD AND COAL sheds are very common but not always recognised. They are low rectangular buildings with the doorway the full height of the wall. They often adjoin the brewhouse. Occasionally, as at Milbourne Farm, Corsham, they are architect-designed as part of a model farm.

Fuel stores; May's Farm, Hullavington (left), and Stanley Abbey Farm, Bremhill (right)

Fuel stores; Church Farm, Great Hinton (timber-framed) (left) and Milbourne Farm, Corsham (right).

Old equipment

MUCH OF THE equipment used on farms was made either on the farm or by local makers. In the 19th century waggons, carts and agricultural equipment and machinery of all kinds were made by, for example, Carson and Toone of Warminster, R. and J. Reeves of Bratton Iron Works, Maudrells of Calne and Brown and May of Devizes. William Cambridge, who moved to Lavington Iron Works, Market Lavington in 1841, invented the press wheel roller and clod crusher for compacting light land and breaking up clods. He also designed and built portable steam engines. Churns and other dairy equipment were made by Hathaways of Chippenham.

Shepherd's huts

IN THE 19TH century the shepherds lived in wheeled huts which were moved from place to place when the sheep were on the downs. They provided sleeping accommodation, especially during lambing, somewhere to keep equipment and protection for sick or orphaned lambs. Many were supplied by local makers including R. and J. Reeves and Coombe Bissett Steam Plough Works.

Early examples were made of wood. Later examples had a wooden chassis on cast iron wheels with a roof and walls of corrugated iron, panelled with wood inside. The interior usually had a table, stool, bed and a small stove for heating and cooking. Some had only a stove.

Shepherd's huts: formerly at Manor Farm, Burcombe Without (left), made by George Farris at the Steam Plough Works, Combe Bissett, the shafts replaced by a tractor draw bar, and at Catridge Farm, Lacock (right).

Stove and chimney in a hut at New Farm, Lacock.

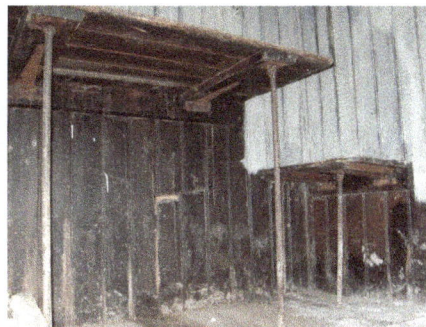

Wheel of a shepherd's hut at Chitterne Manor, Chitterne made by Reeves of Bratton. A bench and table, part of the interior fold away furniture.

Miscellaneous other equipment

Plough.

Seed drill.

Winnowing machines.

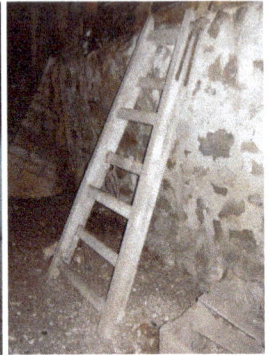

Cake crackers, belt driven from shafting. Extendable ladder.

Sack winch. Water pump. Scythe.

Cider press.   *Double cheese press.*   *Cattle crush.*

Hathaway's butter churn and cover.   *Hay sledge.*   *Churn.*

Churn washer.   *Grindstones.*

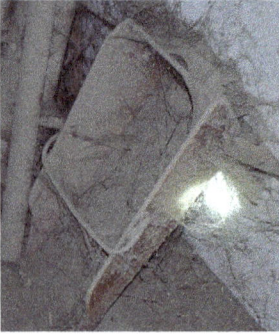

Grain scoop.   *Sack trucks.*   *Wheelbarrow.*

see panel opposite

Suggested Further Reading

General

J. H. Bettey **'Rural Life in Wessex 1500-1900'** Alan Sutton 1987

R. Brigden **'Victorian Farms'** Crowood Press 1986

R. W. Brunskill **'Traditional Farm Buildings of Britain'** Phillimore 1988

G. E. Fussell 'The Farmer's Tools' Bloomsbury Books 1952

English Heritage **'National Farm Building Types'** English Heritage 2013

N. Harvey **'A History of Farm Buildings in England and Wales'** David and Charles 1984

J. E. C. Peters **'Discovering Traditional Farm Buildings'** Shire Publications 1981

S. Wade Martins **'Historic Farm Buildings'** Batsford 1991

S Wade Martins 'The English Model Farm - building the agricultural ideal 1700-1914' Windgather Press 2002

Wiltshire

J.H. Bettey 'Rural Life in Wessex 1500-1900' Alan Sutton 1987

J. H. Bettey 'The Development of Agriculture' in M. Corfield **'Industrial Archaeology of Wiltshire'** WCC 1978

J.H. Bettey **'Wiltshire Farming in the Seventeenth Century'** Wiltshire Record Society, vol. 57, 2005

J. Collins and J. Flanagan **'Stanley Abbey Farm, Bremhill'** Wiltshire Buildings Record, 2023

M. Corfield **'A Guide to the Industrial Archaeology of Wiltshire'** WCC for WANHS 1978

E. Crittall **'Victoria County History of Wiltshire'** vol. 4, OUP 1959 (section on agriculture)

T. Davis **'General View of the Agriculture of Wiltshire'** 1794 and 1811

B. Edwards and J. Lake **'Wiltshire & Swindon Farmsteads and Landscape Project for English Heritage and Wiltshire Buildings Record'** Forum Heritage Services 2014

A. Foster **'Beeboles and Bee Houses'** Shire Classic 204, 2010

G. Grigson **'An English Farmhouse and Its Neighbourhood'** Max Parrish and Co Ltd 1948

1950s dairy equipment; Alfa Laval vacuum pipeline and pressure gauge (top left), butter churn (top right), cooler (mid left), butter churn (mid right). milk pan (bottom left) which stood on top of the cooler and allowed the milk to flow down at a speed regulated by the tap, milk strainer (bottom right) which stood on top of the churn.

John Hare 'A Prospering Society - Wiltshire in the later Middle Ages' University of Hertfordshire Press 2011

S. Hobbs 'Wiltshire Glebe Terriers 1588-1827' WRS, vol. 56

A. Ingram 'Dairying Bygones' Shire Album 29, 1977 (The author lived at Devizes)

R. Jefferies 'The Toilers of the Field' Futura 1981 reprint

R. Jefferies 'Hodge and His Masters' Faber and Faber 1946 reprint (Many of Jefferies' other works are also relevant)

E. Kerridge 'Surveys of the Manors of Philip, First Earl of Pembroke and Montgomery 1631-2' Wiltshire Record Society 1953

J. and P. McCann 'Wiltshire Dovecotes and Pigeon Lofts' Hobnob Press for Wiltshire Buildings Record, 2011

R. P de B. Nicholson, articles in *Wiltshire Folk Life*; vol. 1, no 2 Cart shed, vol. 1, no 3 Farm Buildings, vol. 2 No 1 Cider Mill and Barns, vol. 2, no 3 Barns, Granaries and Staddle Stones

M. Reeves 'Sheep Bell and Ploughshare' Paladin 1980 (about Bratton)

P. M. and I. M. Slocombe 'The Buildings of Barton Farm, Bradford-on-Avon' Ex Libris Press for Bradford-on-Avon Museum 2016

P. M. Slocombe 'Whaddon and the Longs – A West Wiltshire History' Hobnob Press 2020 (sections on farming in the area between Melksham and Trowbridge, medieval to 19th century)

P. Stanier 'Wiltshire in the Age of Steam' Halsgrove 2006 (especially chapters on 'Farming in the Industrial Age' and ' Foundries and Engineering')

A. Wadsworth 'Pastoral and Arable : Contrasts from Wiltshire' in *Vernacular Architecture,* vol. 47 for 2016 (general discussion of Wiltshire farms followed by case studies of a pastoral farm at Lacock and an arable farm at Maiden Bradley)

A. Wadsworth 'The Farming Diaries of Thomas Pinniger 1813-1847' WRS vol. 74 (farming at Little Bedwyn, Chippenham and Beckhampton)

A. R. Wilson 'Cocklebury : a farming area and its people in the Vale of Wiltshire' Phillimore 1983 (a dairy farm at Chippenham)

A. R. Wilson 'Forgotten Harvest' Ex Libris Press 1995 (describing the cheese industry)

A. R. Wilson 'Forgotten Labour' Hobnob Press 2007 (describing the life of the farm labourer)

Historic Farm Buildings Group This national group aims to promote the study and appreciation of historic farm buildings. www.hfbg.org.uk

Tree-ring dates Please note that these are the dates of felling but timbers were usually used within a year of felling.

A note about photography

UNTIL ABOUT 2002 all our photography was in black and white with a few additional colour photos and slides. This was because it provided a better lasting and higher quality record. The films were provided by WCC who retained the negatives. We were expected to take only one image per building feature or view. After this date our photography turned to digital which has many advantages especially in the preparation of reports but gives storage problems either on CDs, DVDs or only in the reports or on the office or personal computers etc.

The buildings are photographed as found with a minimum or no disturbance hence a wide variety of 'junk' is on show. This can be frustrating but often includes much original equipment.

We also contend with the light at different times of year and day and varying weather conditions. The recorders are many different people with different skills. The buildings never cease to amaze and interest us and we are grateful to have found so many wonderful places and people.

Acknowledgements

THE WILTSHIRE BUILDINGS Record is indebted to all the people whose farm buildings are included in this book for their cooperation during recording.
Farm buildings recorders: very many people but especially the leaders Nigel Walker, Alan Wadsworth, Tim and Jane Mayhew and Clive Carter.

The Nottingham Tree-ring Laboratory for dendrochronological analysis.

Clive Carter for re-drawing plans.

Endnotes
1 Alcock, Barnwell & Cherry *Cruck Building: a Survey.* 2019
2 H. Stephens *The Book of the Farm,* 1844
3 *Wiltshire Folk Life* vol 1, no 2

www.ingramcontent.com/pod-product-compliance
Lightning Source LLC
Chambersburg PA
CBHW050821090426
42737CB00022B/3461